Nola the Nurse®

Math/English Worksheets for Preschool

Volume 5

by Dr. Scharmaine L. Baker NP

Illustrated by Marvin Alonso

A DrNurse
Publishing House

New Orleans, Louisiana

COPYRIGHT ©2016 by Dr. Scharmaine L. Baker and its licensors.
All rights reserved.

No part of this book may be reproduced or transmitted in any form or by any means, electronic or mechanical, including photocopy, recording, or by any information storage and retrieval system without the written permission of the publisher or author except where permitted by law.

For information address A DrNurse Publishing House
2475 Canal Street, Suite 105, New Orleans, La. 70119
www.NolatheNurse.com

ISBN-13: 978-1-945088-09-4
ISBN-10: 1-945088-09-4

Author Contact info:
DrBakerNP@NolaTheNurse.com

www.DrBakerNP.com
www.NolaTheNurse.com

Beginning Sounds Color it !

www.nolathenurse.com

Color the images that begin with Letter A.

Name : -

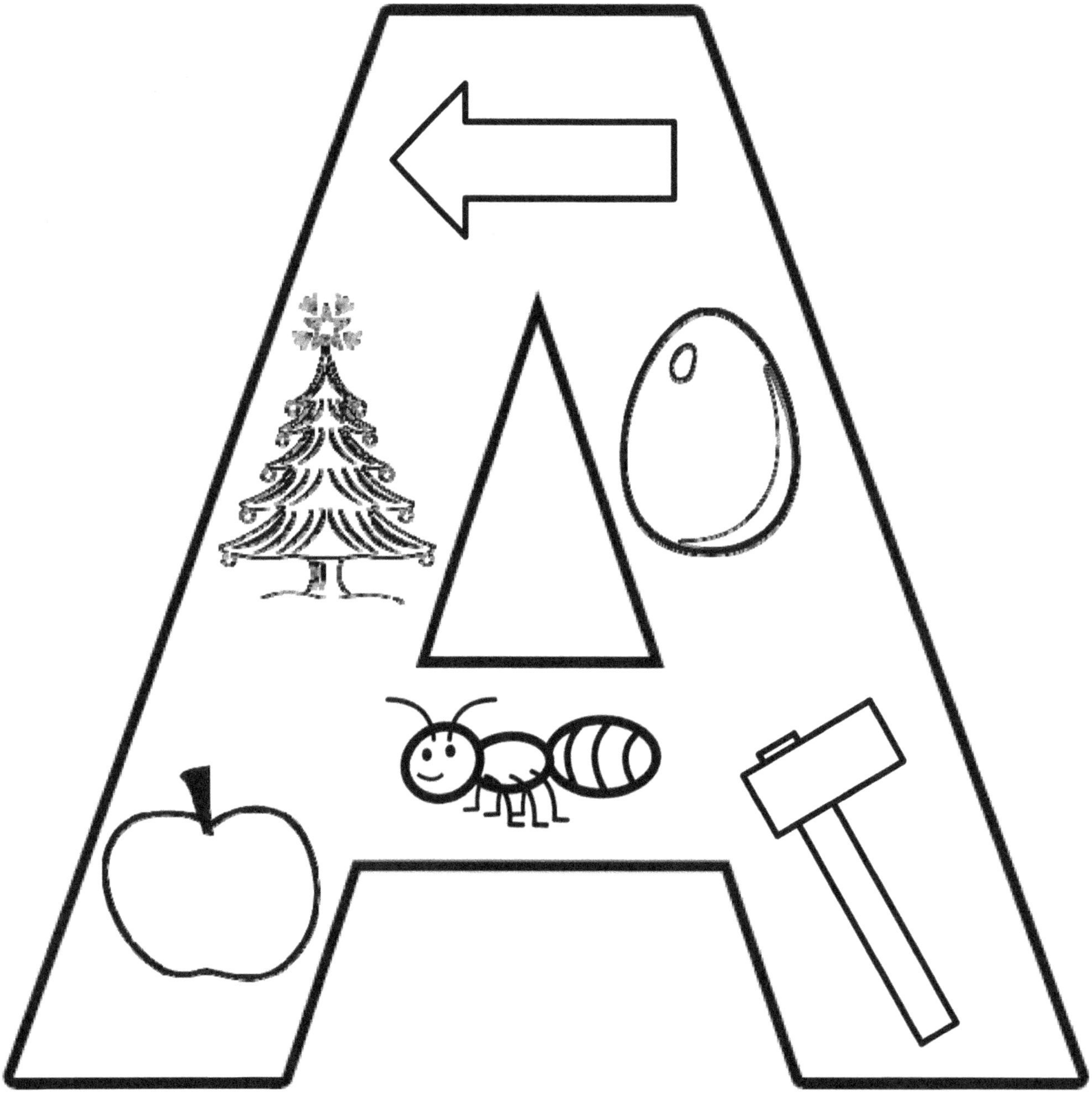

Color the images that begin with Letter B.

Name : -

Color the images that begin with Letter C.

Name : -

Color the images that begin with Letter D.

Name : -

Color the images that begin with Letter E.

Name : -

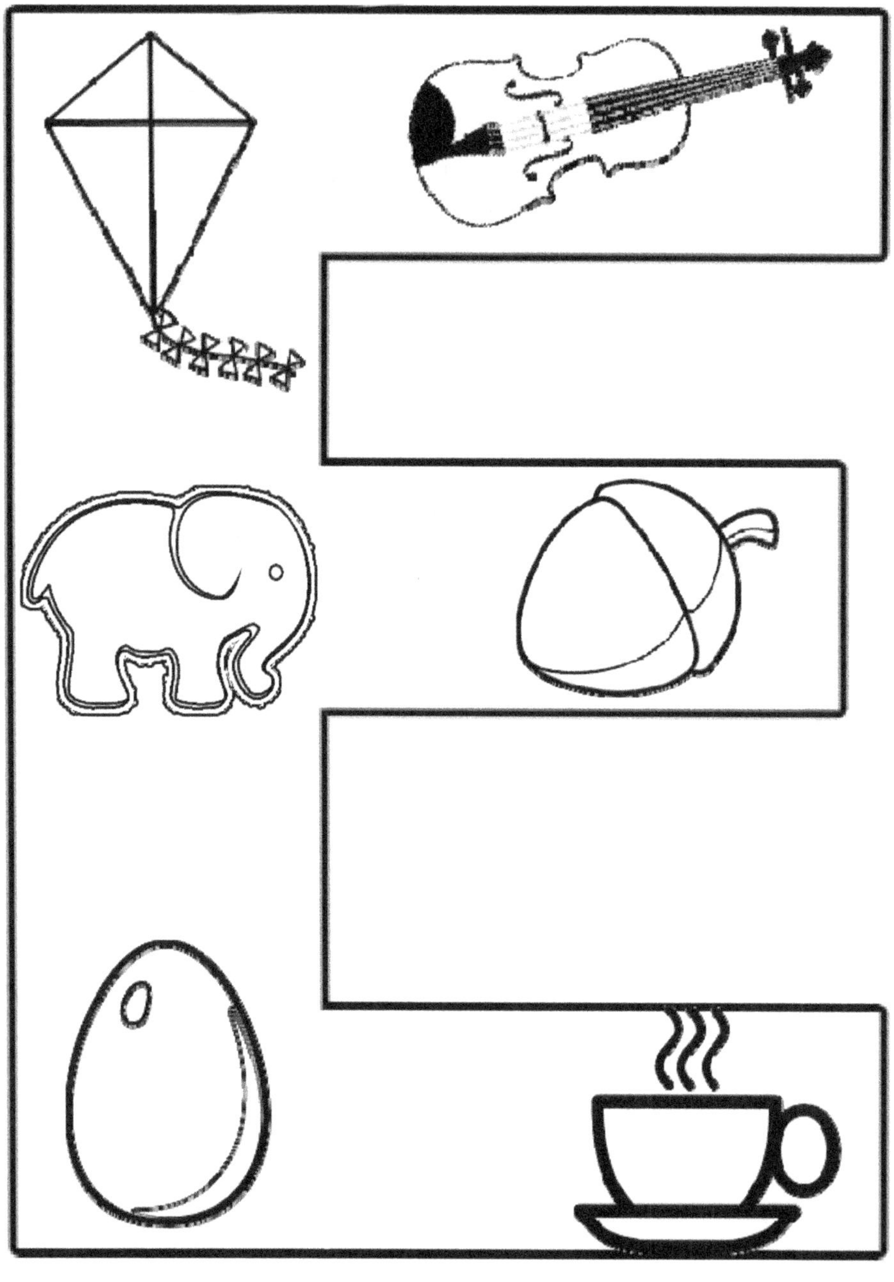

Color the images that begin with Letter F.

Name : -

Color the images that begin with Letter G.

Name : -

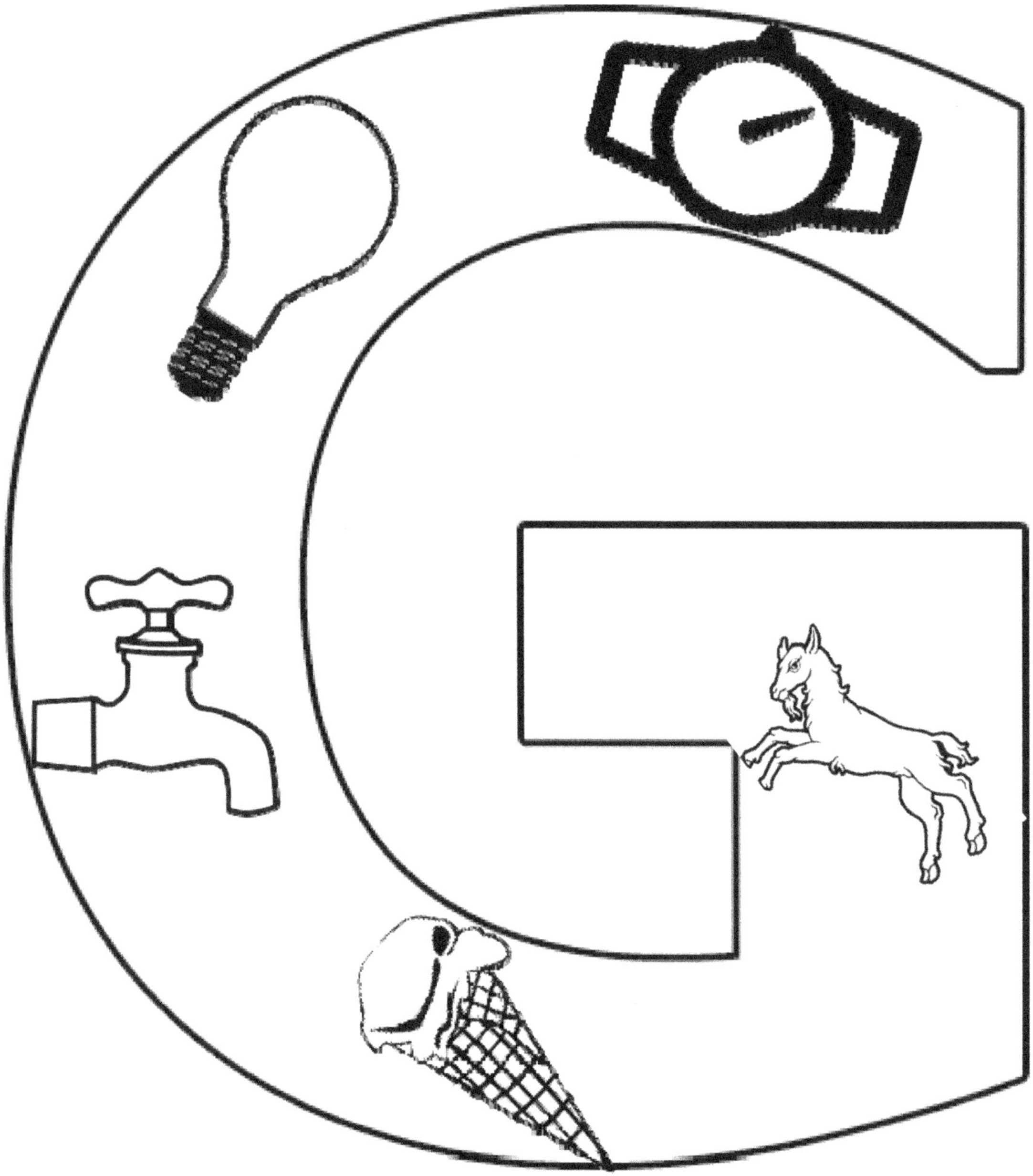

Color the images that begin with Letter F.

Name : -

Color the images that begin with Letter G.

Name : -

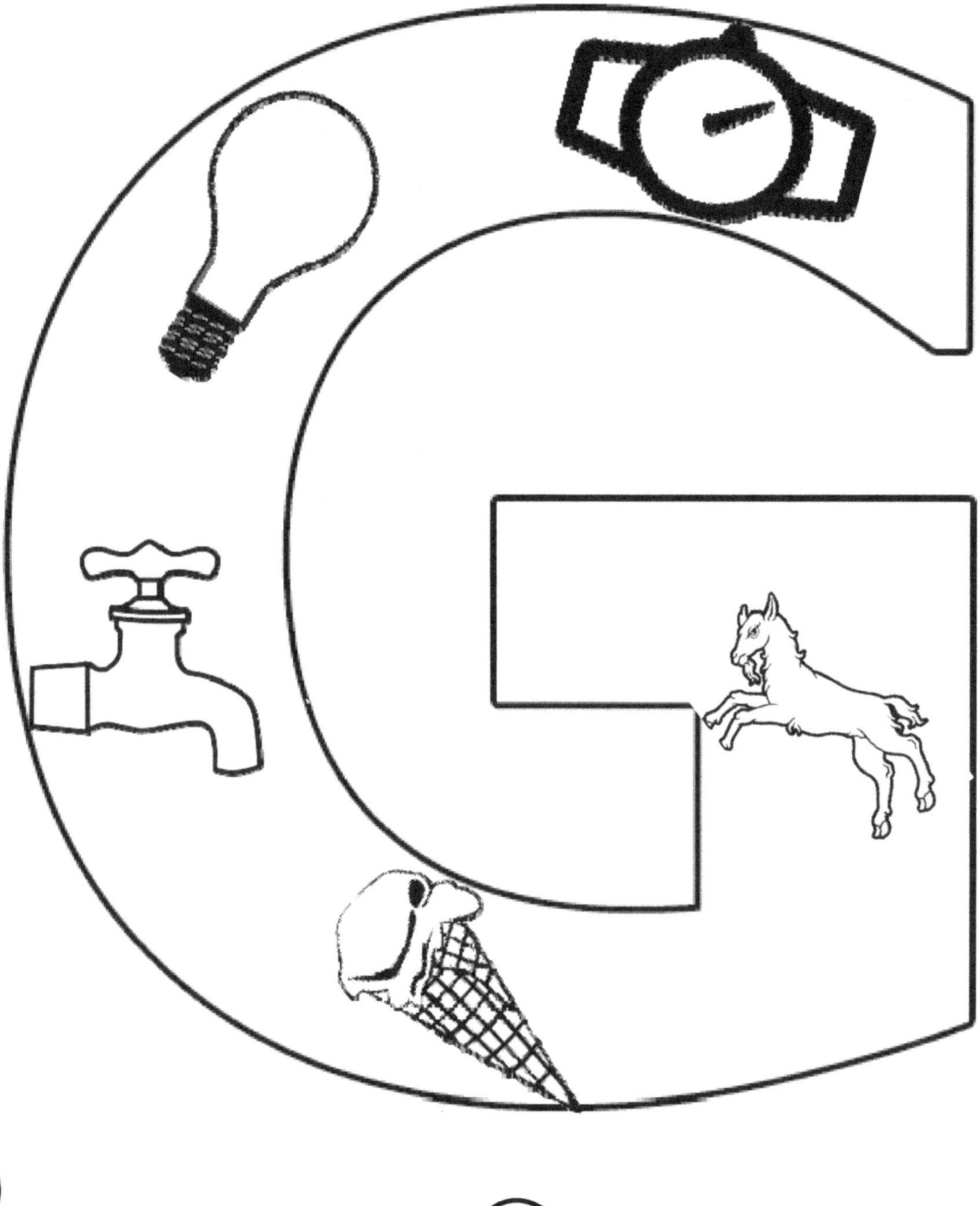

www.nolathenurse.com

Color the images that begin with Letter H.

Name : -

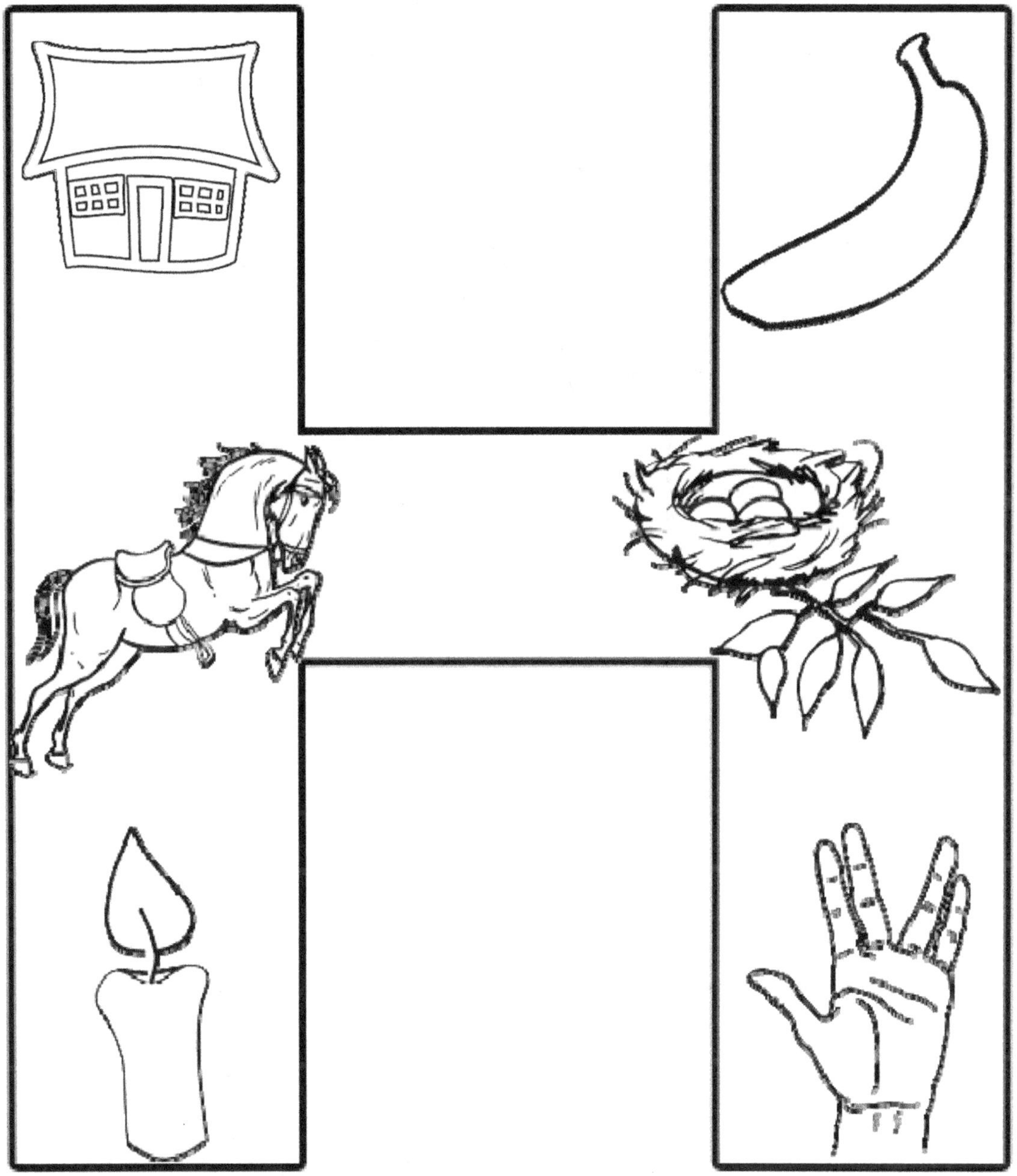

Color the images that begin with Letter I.

Name : -

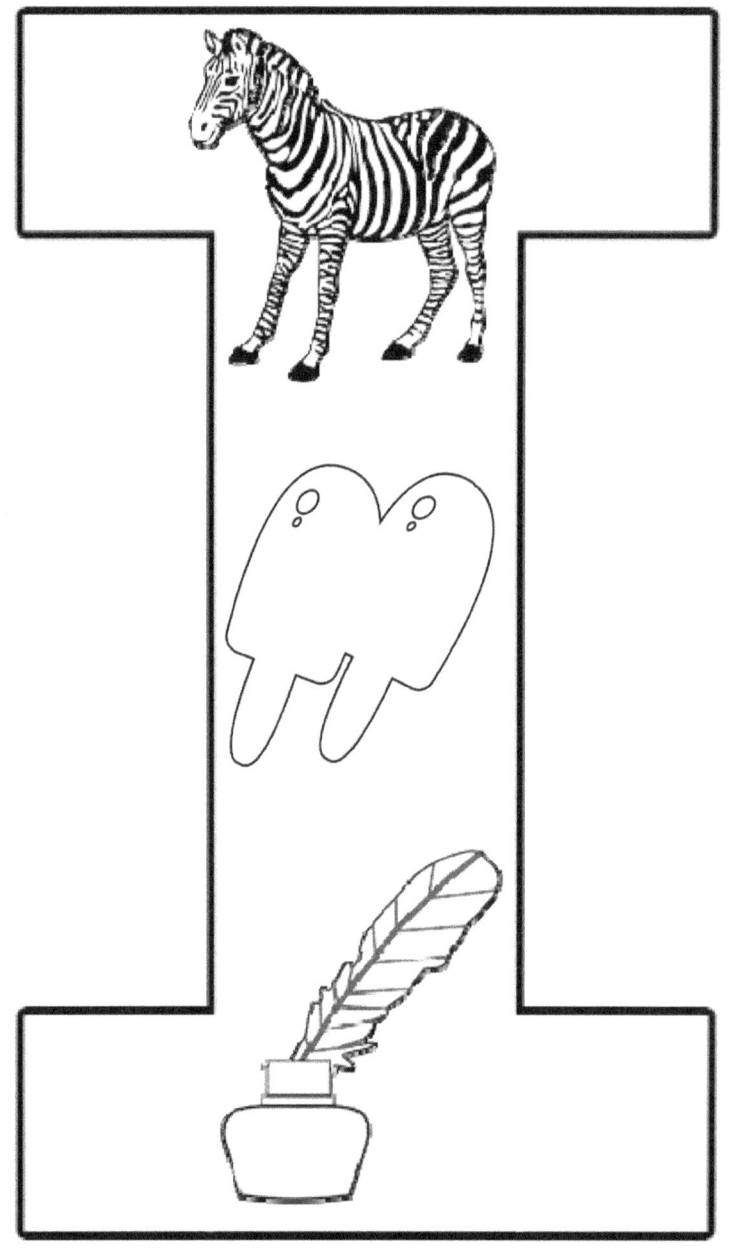

Color the images that begin with Letter J.

Name : -

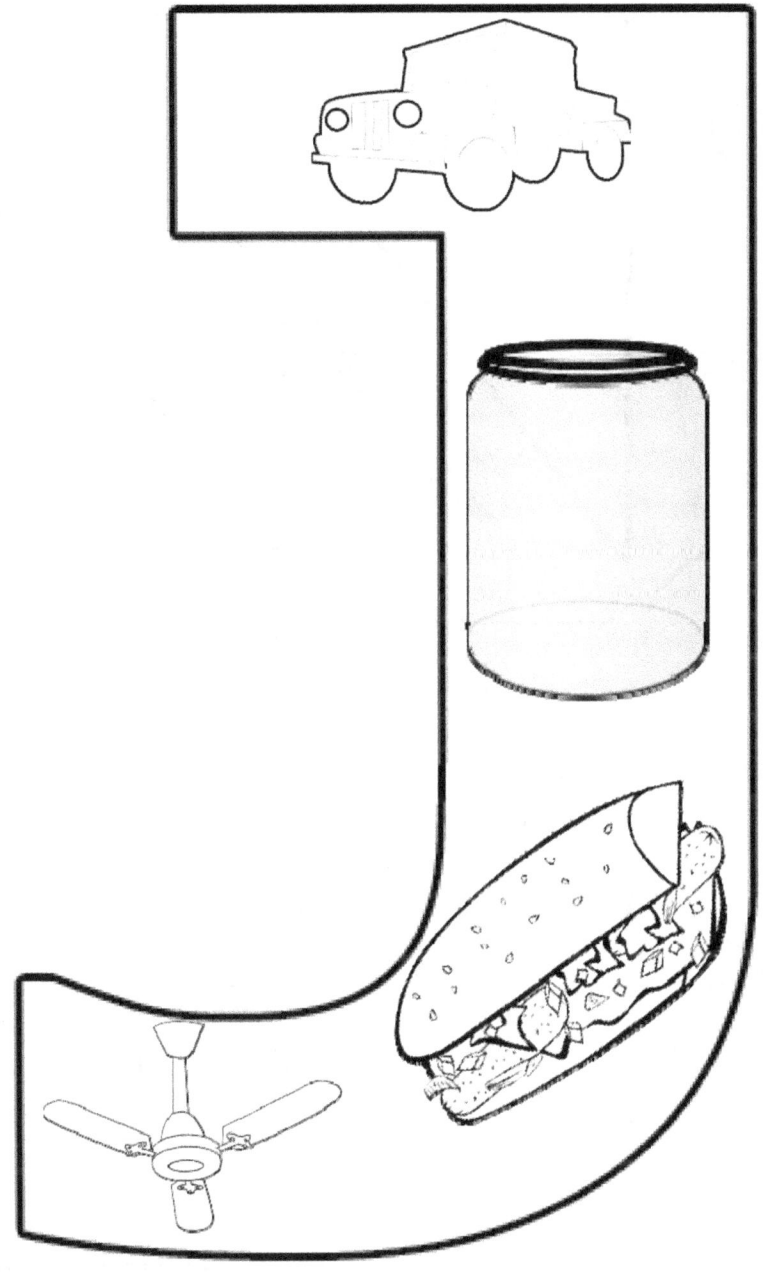

Color the images that begin with Letter K.

Name : -

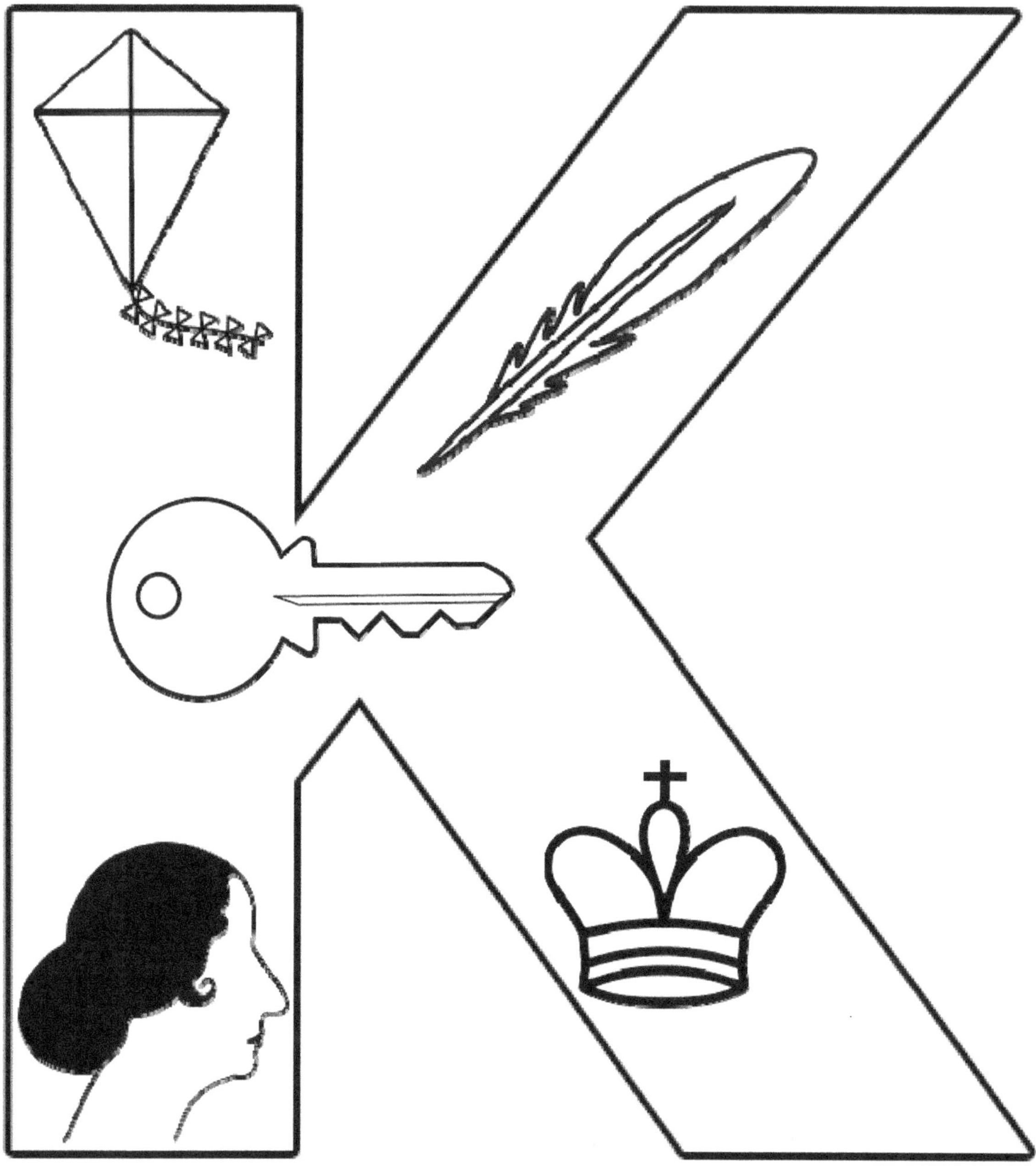

Color the images that begin with Letter L.

Name : -

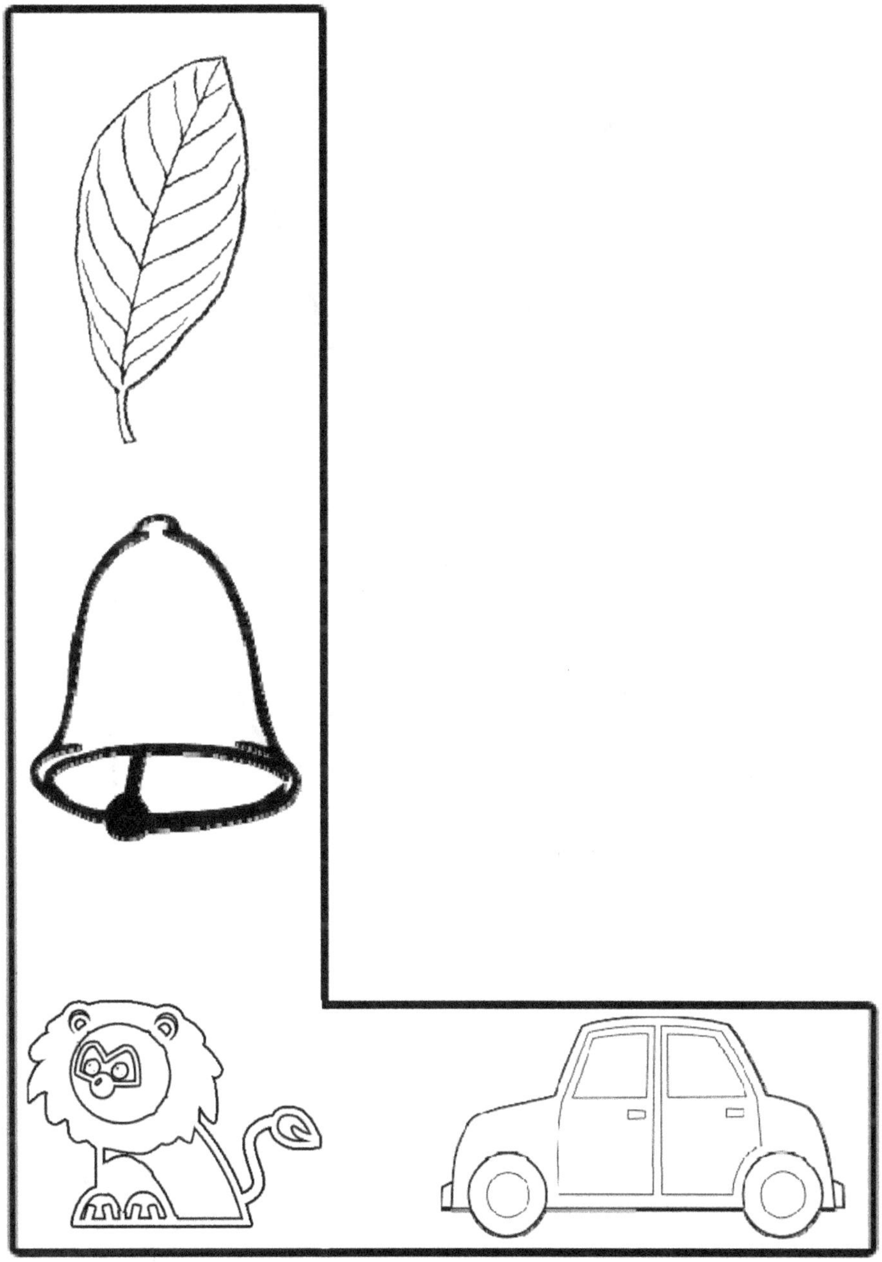

Color the images that begin with Letter M.

Name : -

www.nolathenurse.com

Color the images that begin with Letter N.

Name : -

Color the images that begin with Letter O.

Name : -

Color the images that begin with Letter R.

Name : -

Color the images that begin with Letter S.

Name : -

Color the images that begin with Letter T.

Name : -

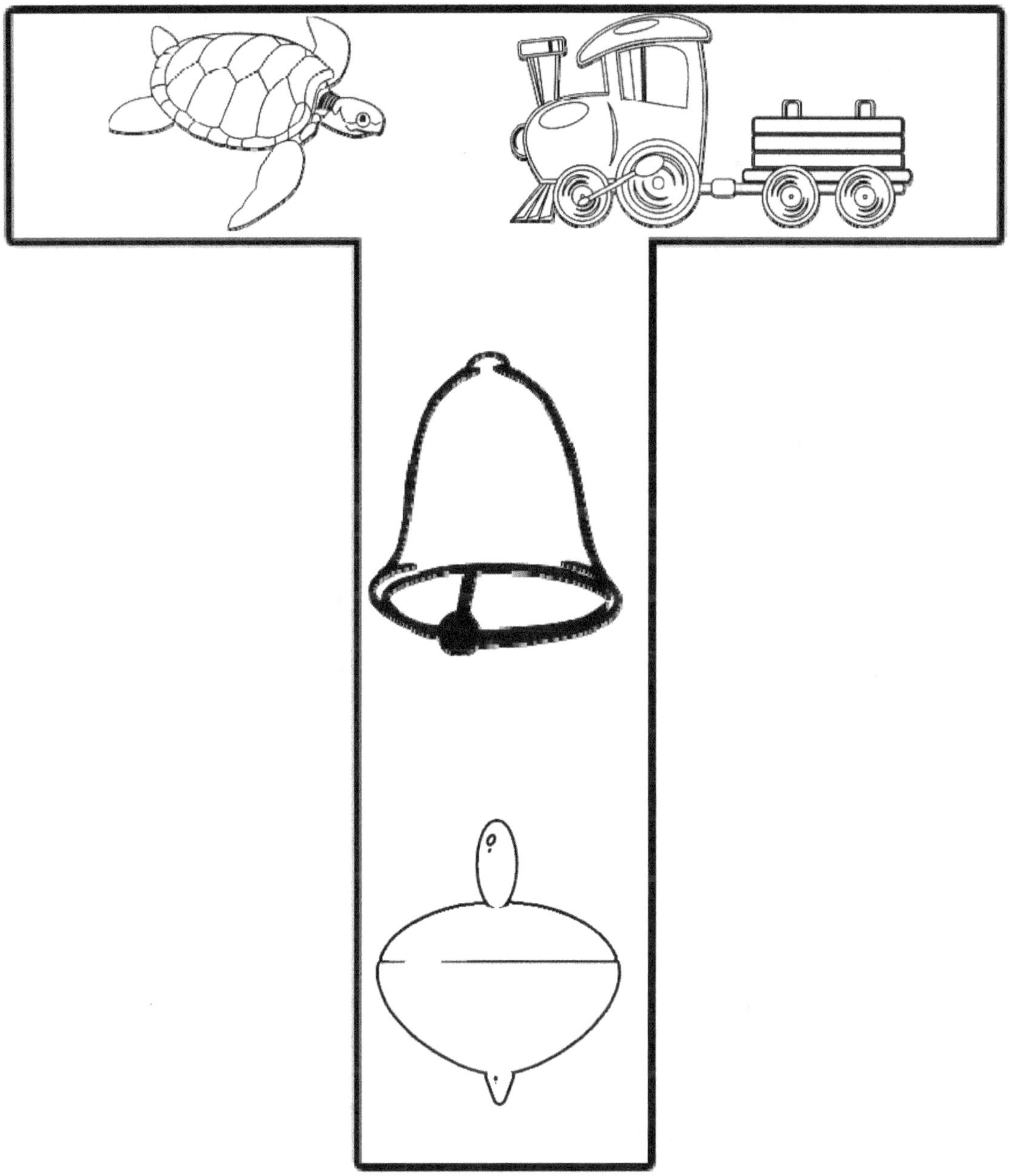

Color the images that begin with Letter U.

Name : -

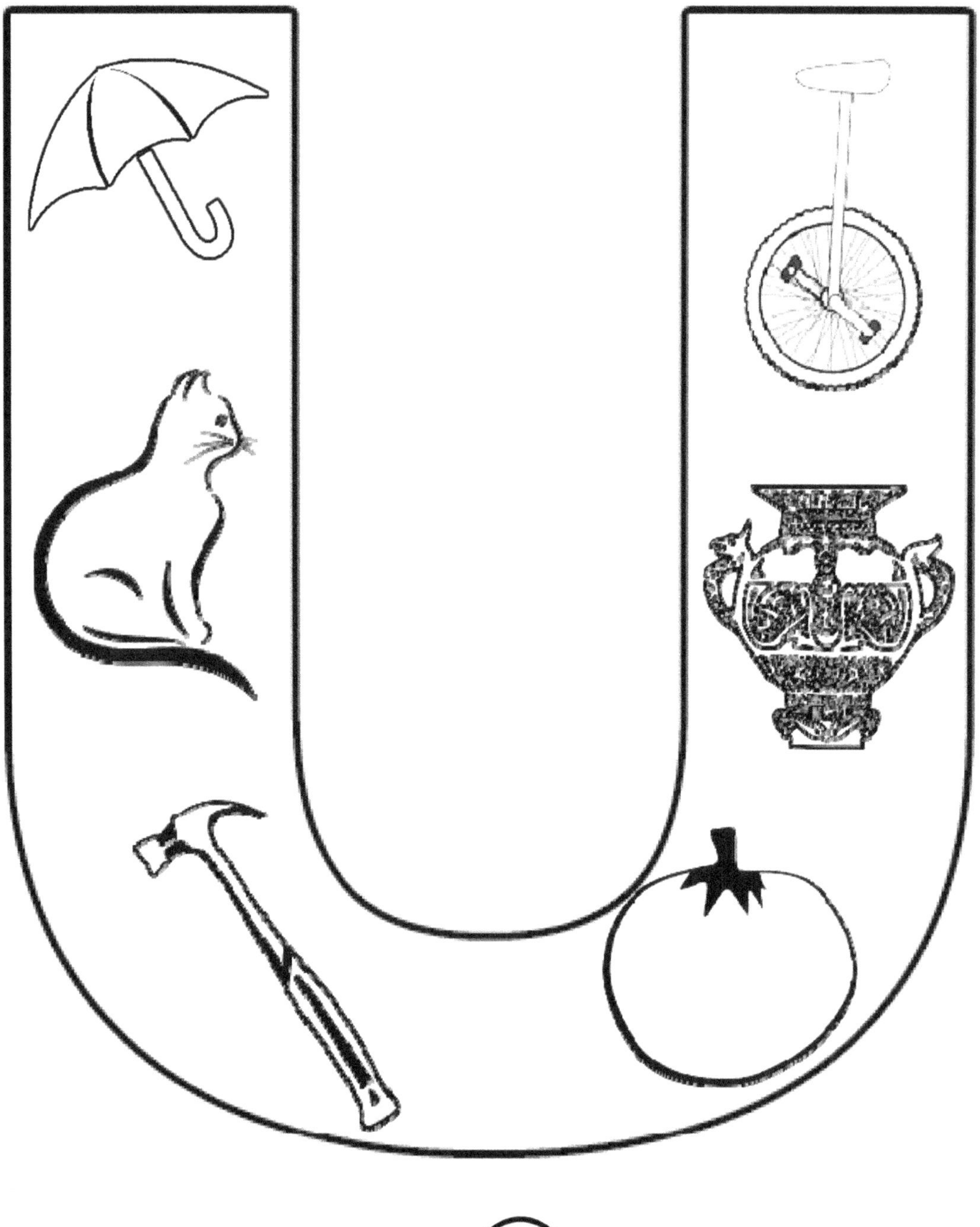

Color the images that begin with Letter V.

Name : -

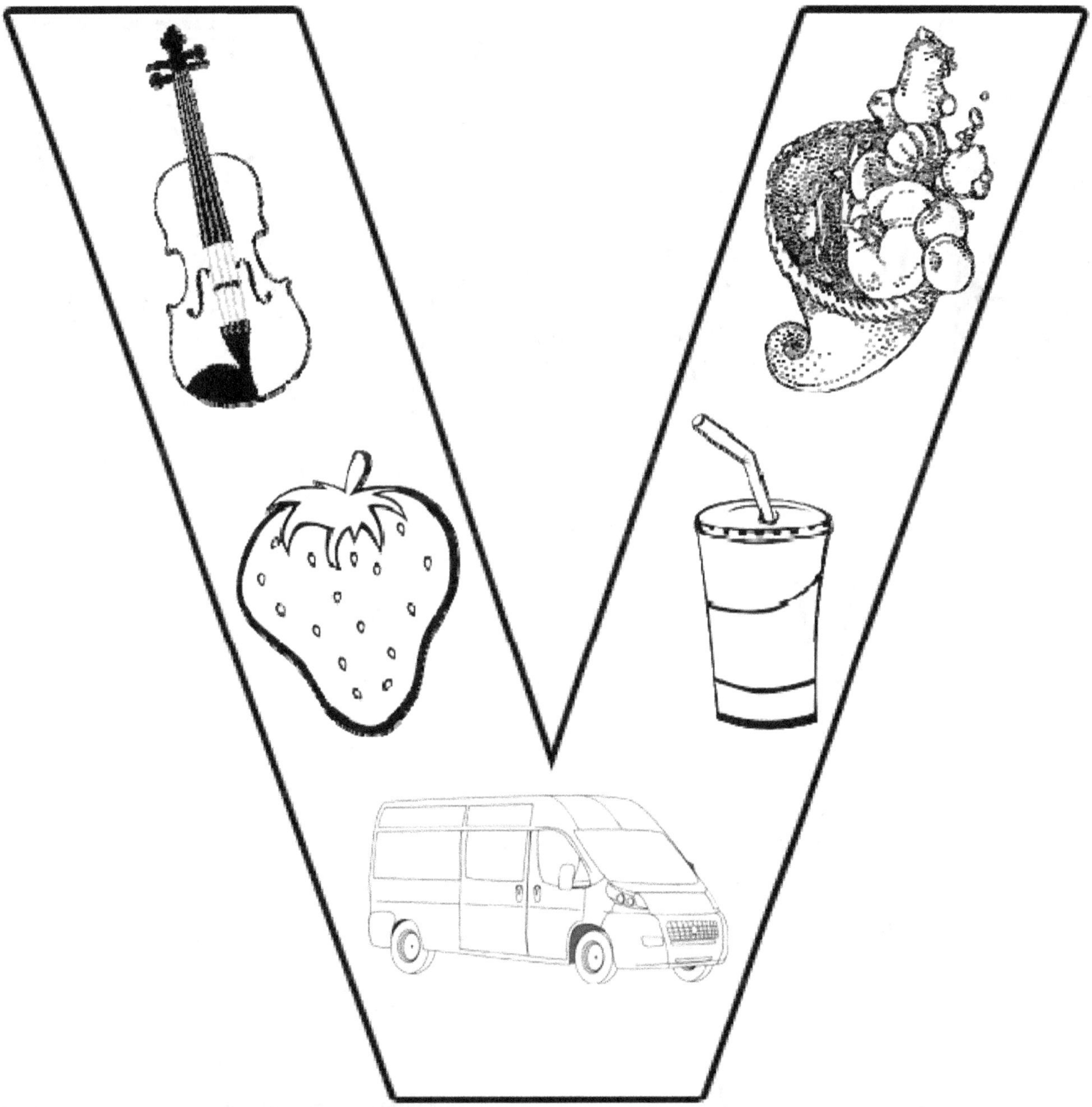

Color the images that begin with Letter W.

Name : -

Color the images that begin with Letter X.

Name : -

Color the images that begin with Letter Y.

Name : -

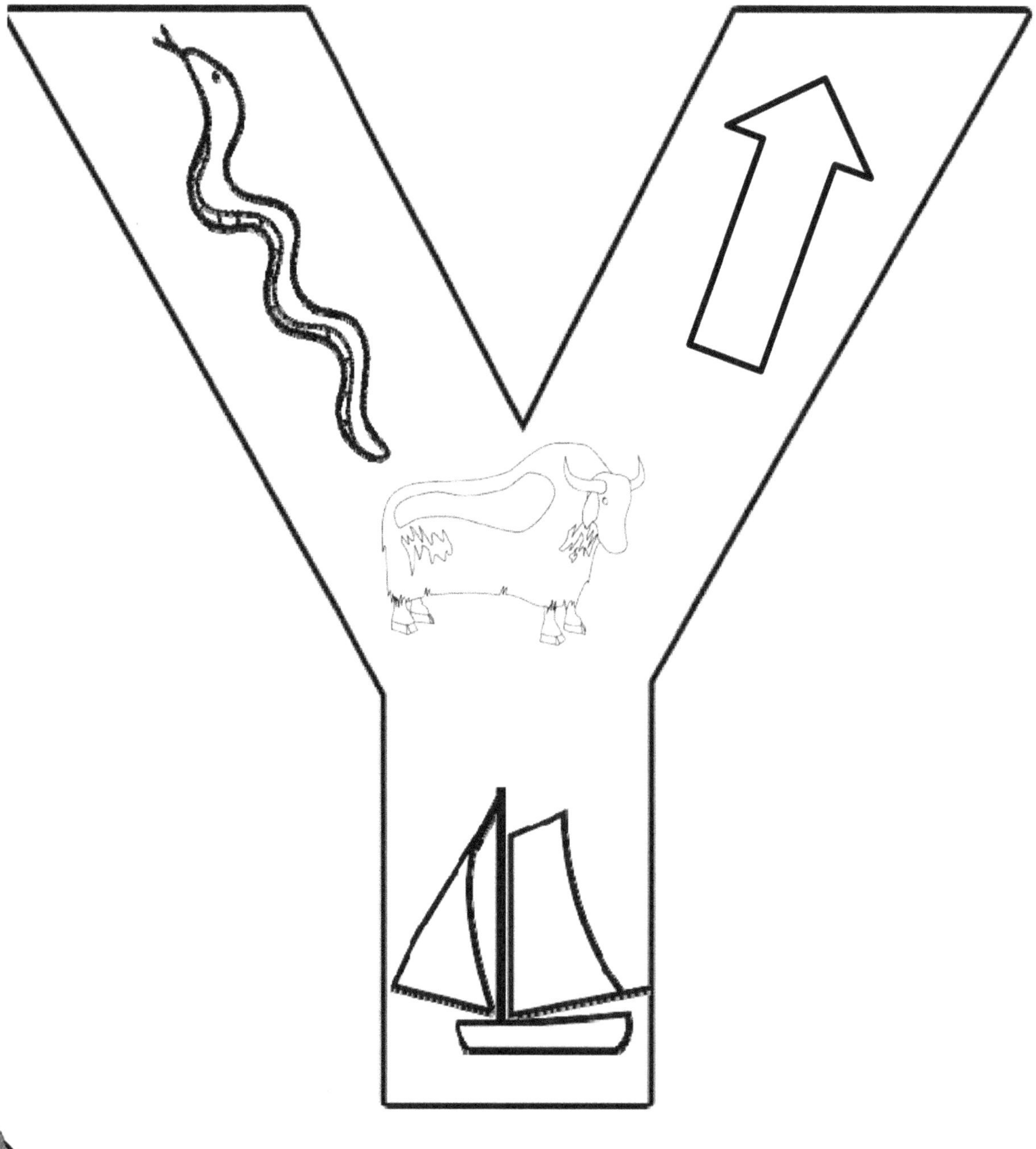

Color the images that begin with Letter Z.

Name : -

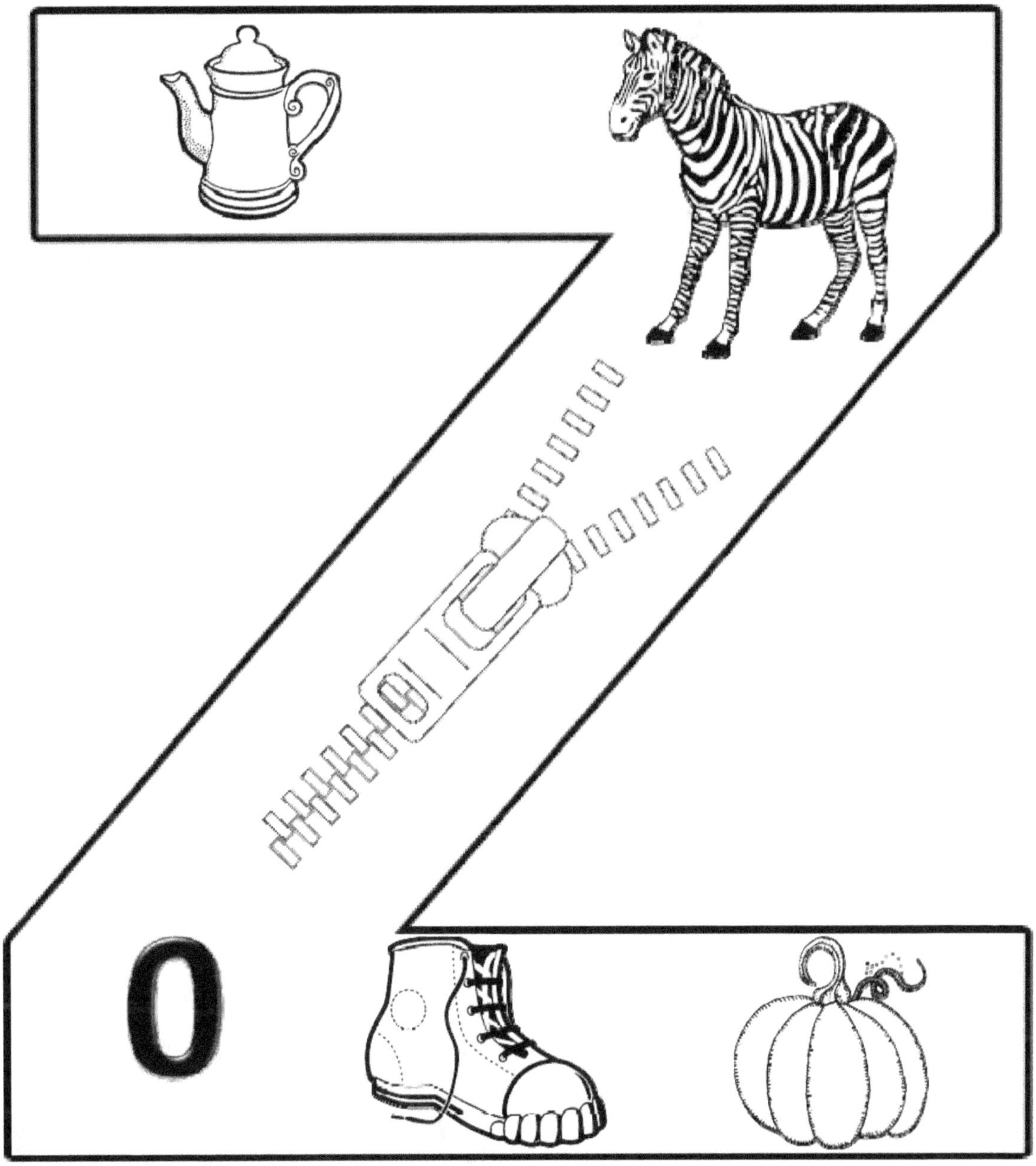

Activity sheet Letter A.

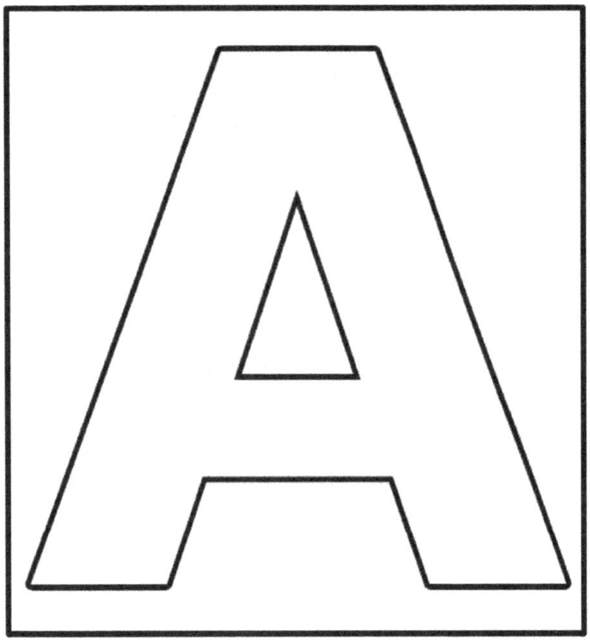

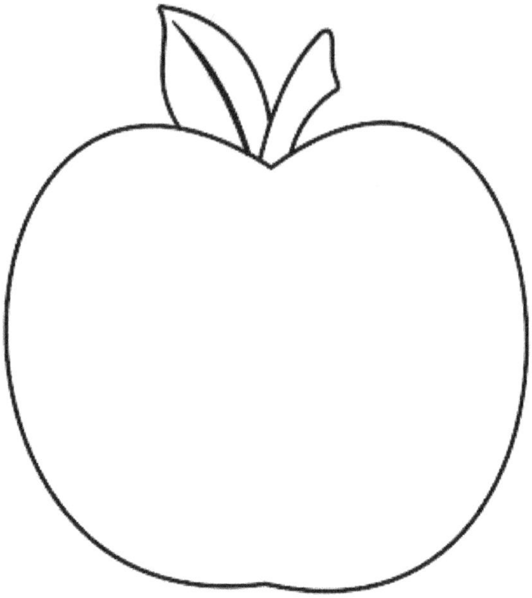

A | L | A | M

F | A | U | C

X | A | O | A

A | P | A | Z

Activity sheet Letter B.

Activity sheet Letter C.

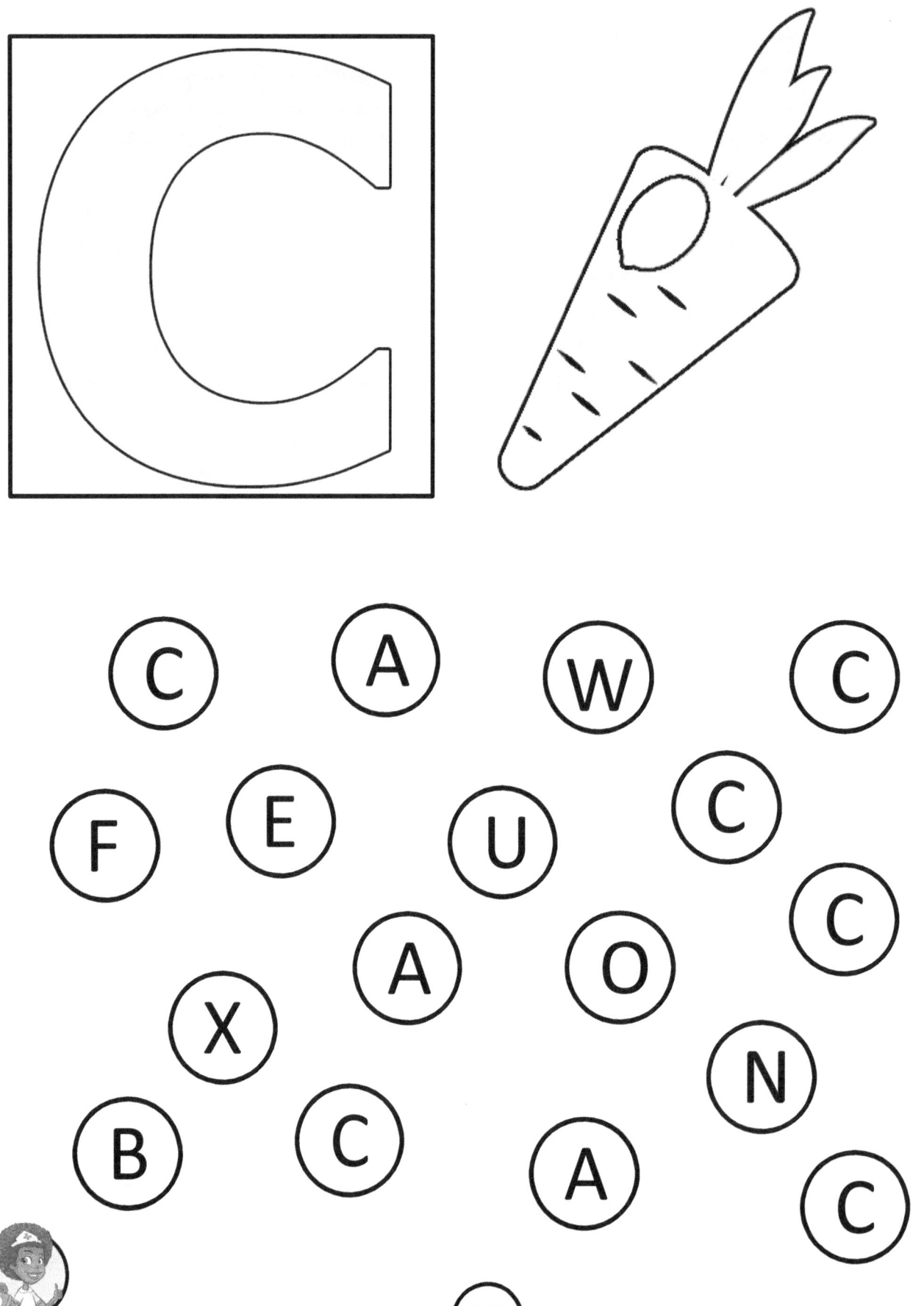

Activity sheet Letter D.

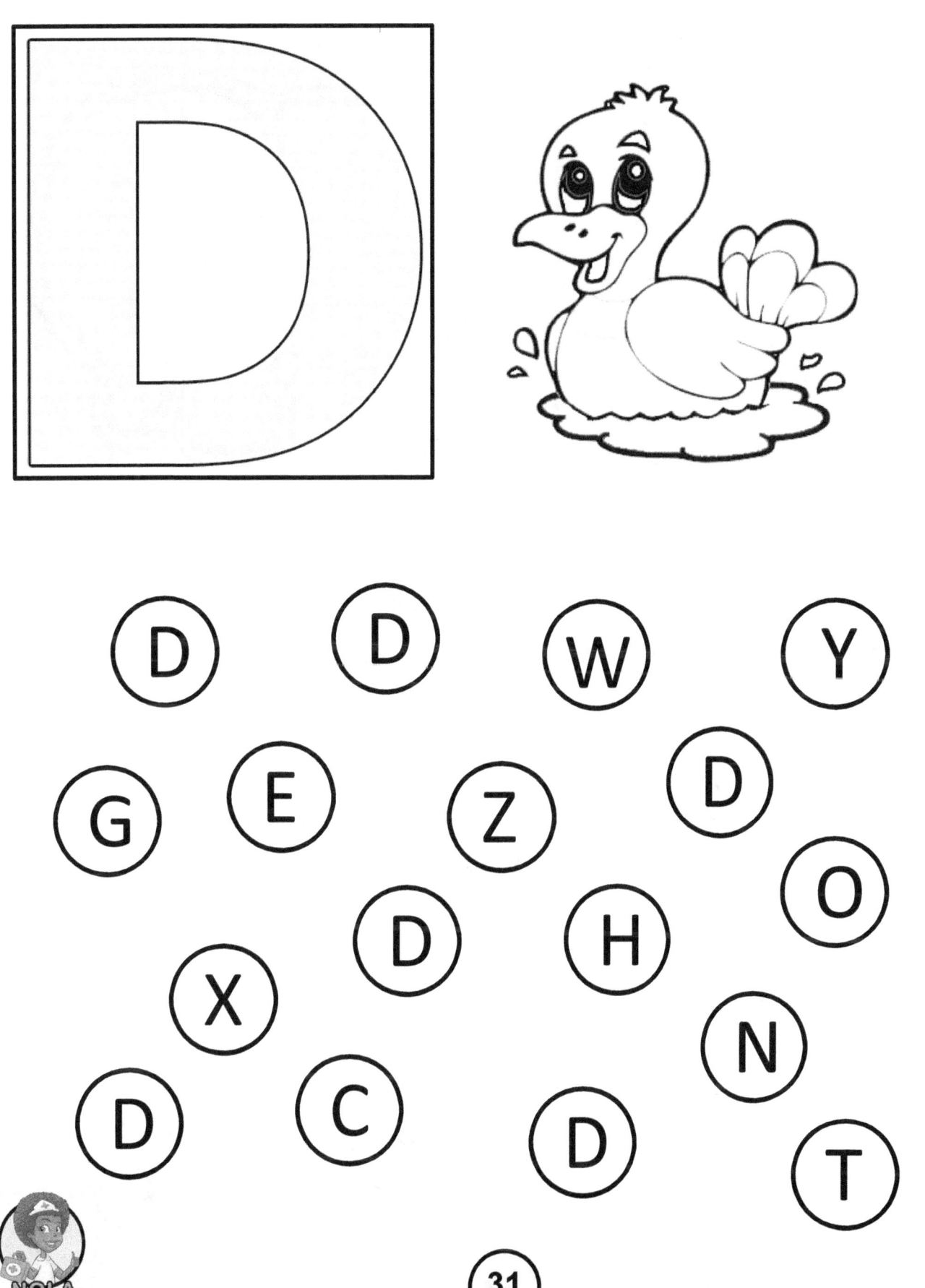

Activity sheet Letter E.

Activity sheet Letter F.

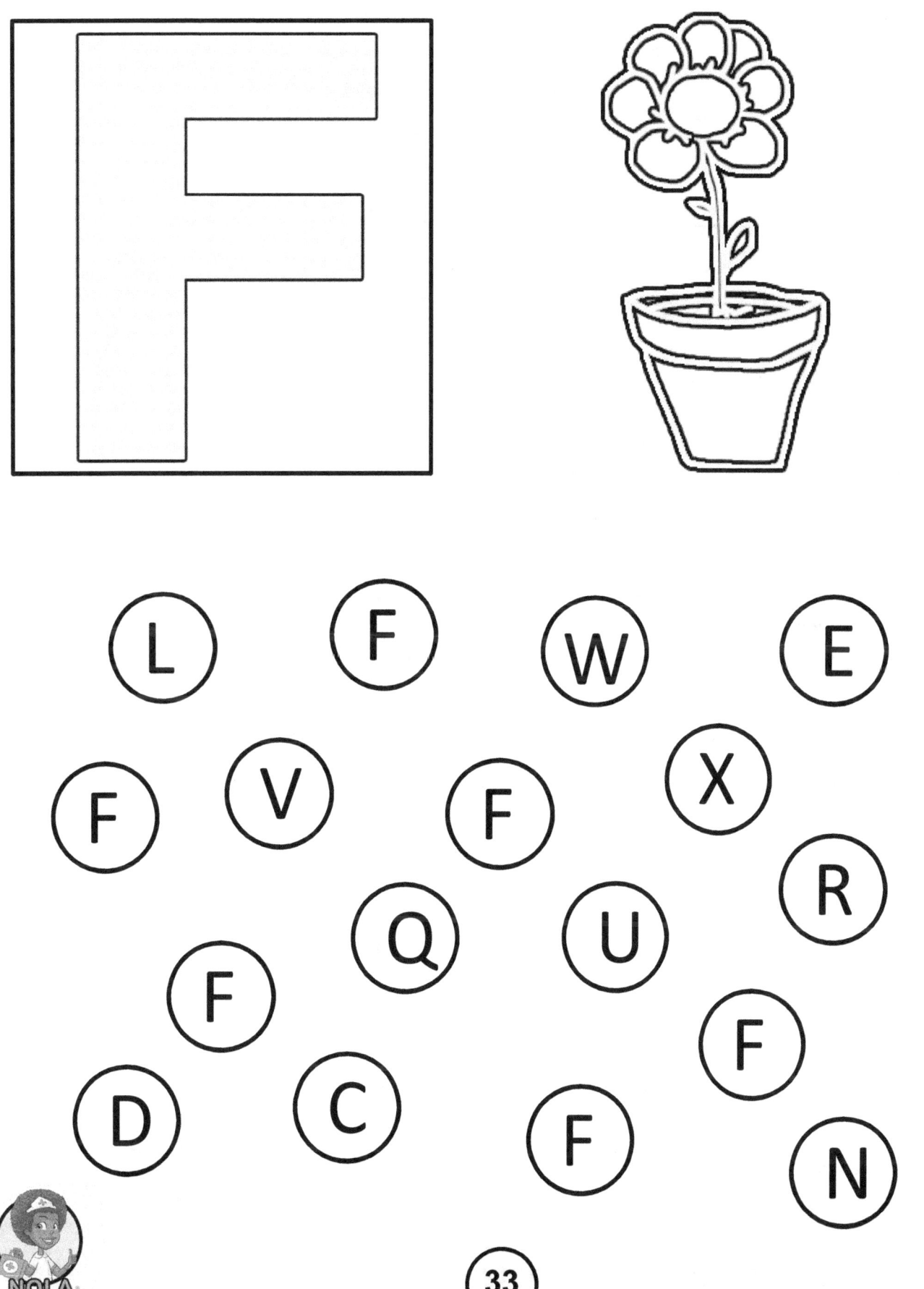

Activity sheet Letter G.

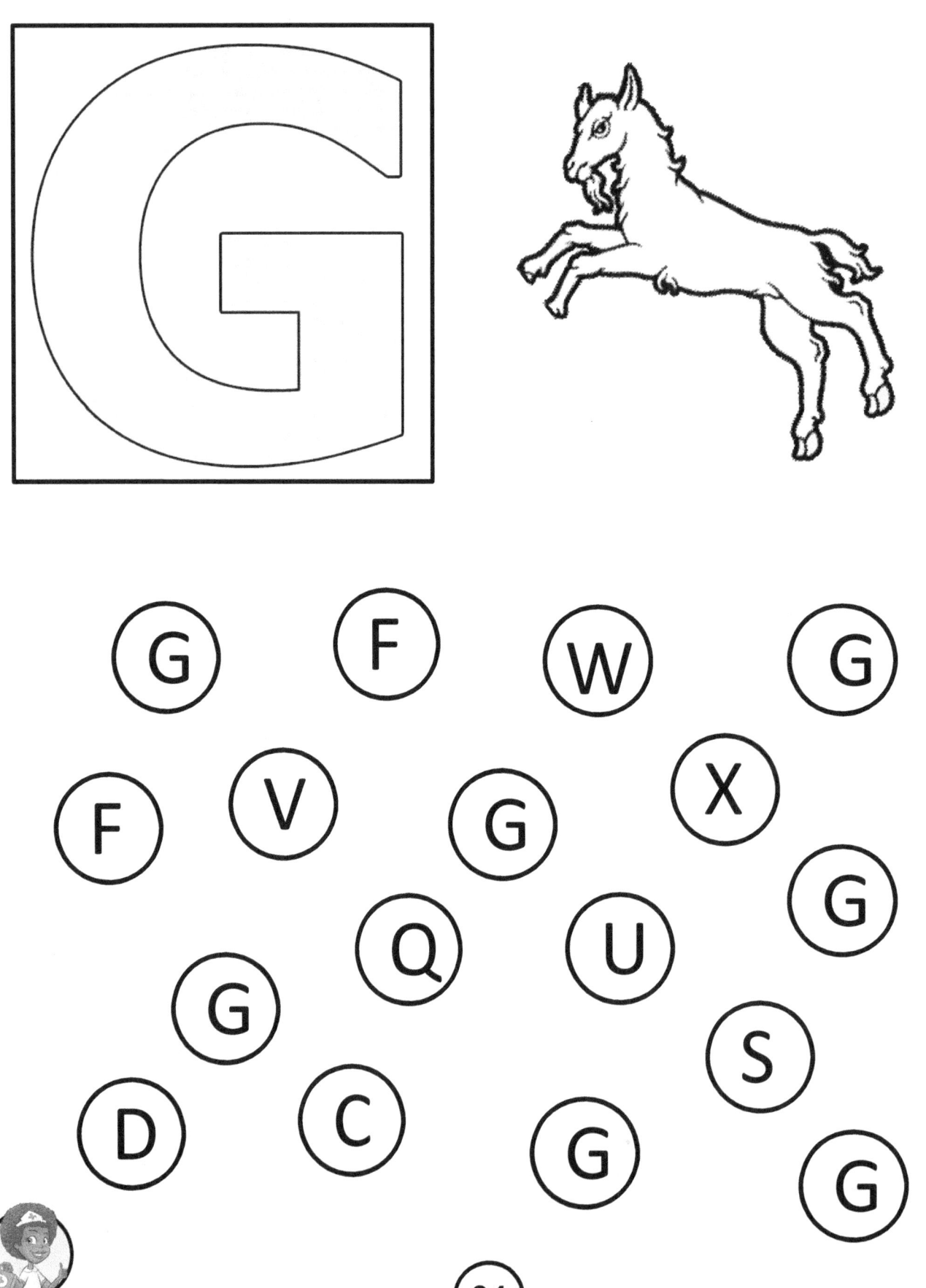

Activity sheet Letter H.

Activity sheet Letter I.

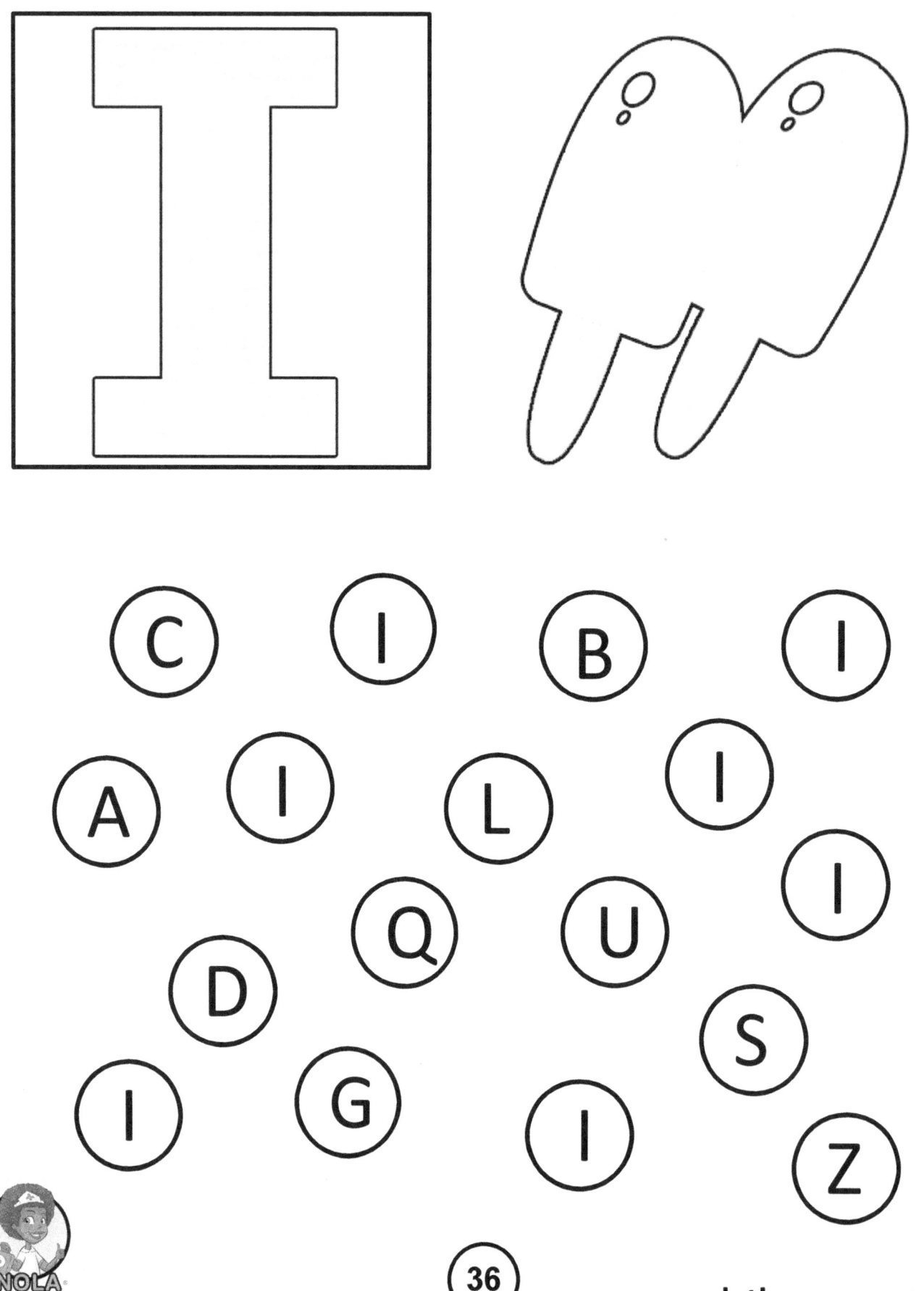

Activity sheet Letter J.

Activity sheet Letter K.

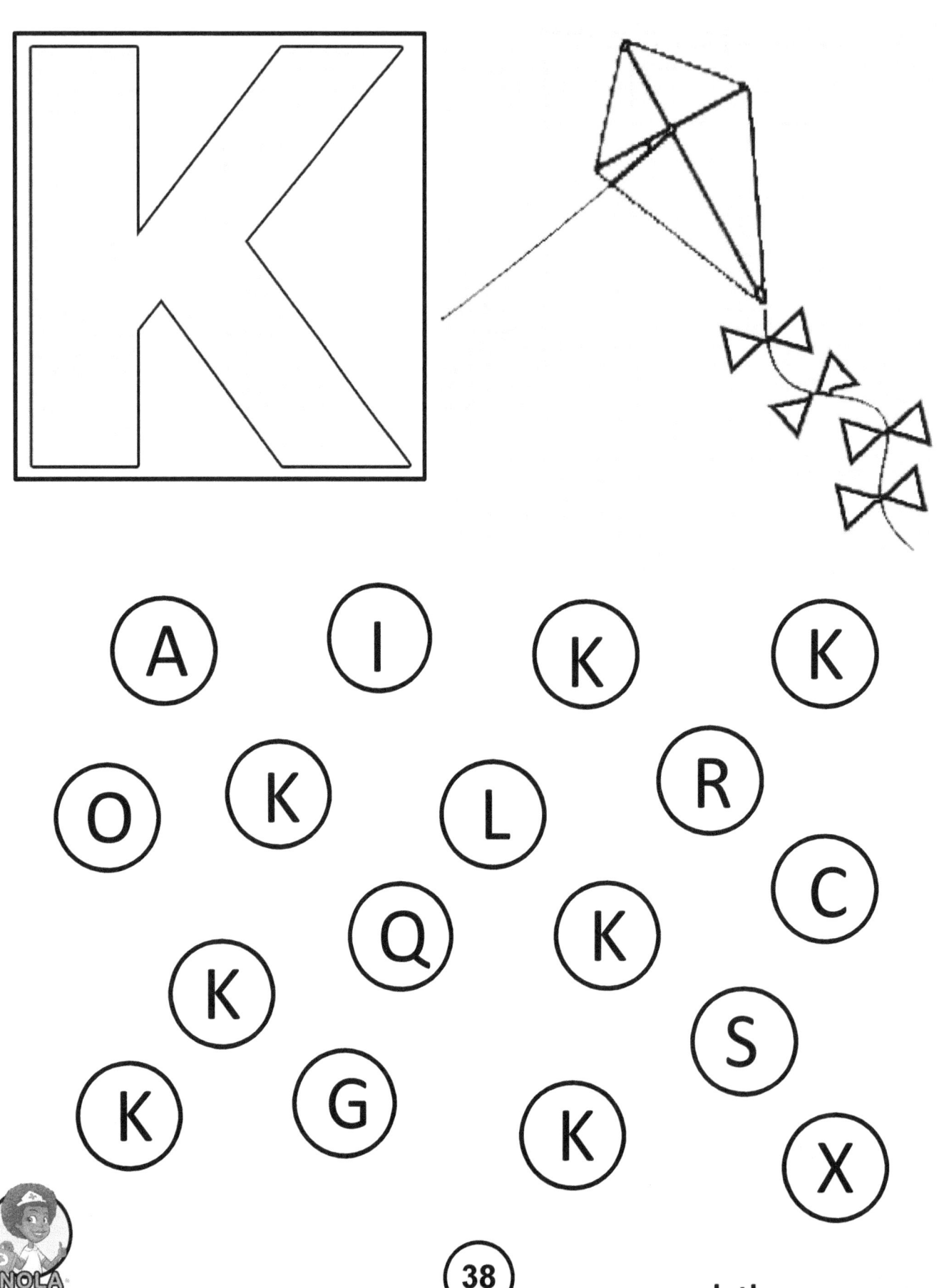

38

www.nolathenurse.com

Activity sheet Letter L.

Activity sheet Letter M.

Activity sheet Letter N.

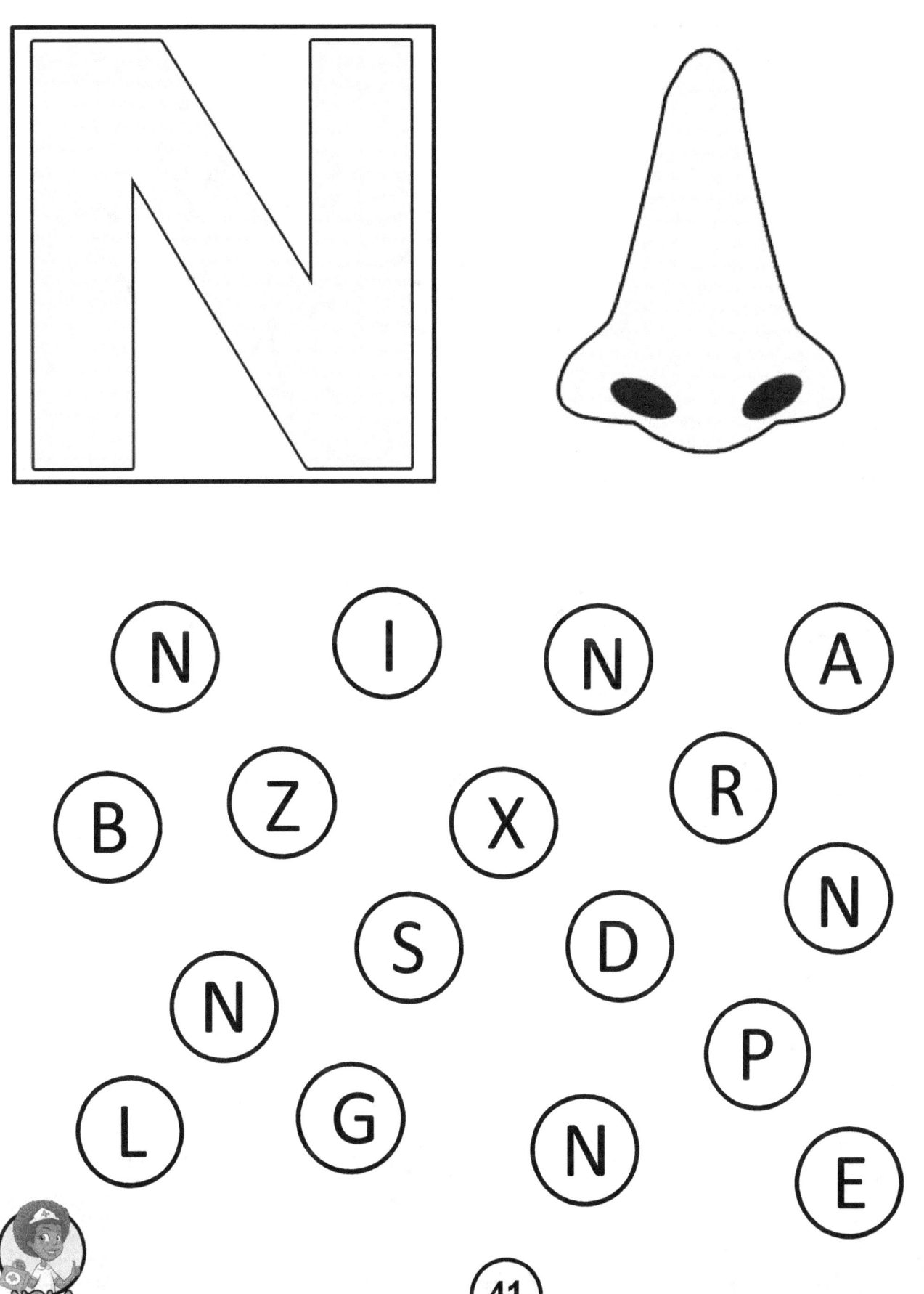

Activity sheet Letter O.

Activity sheet Letter P.

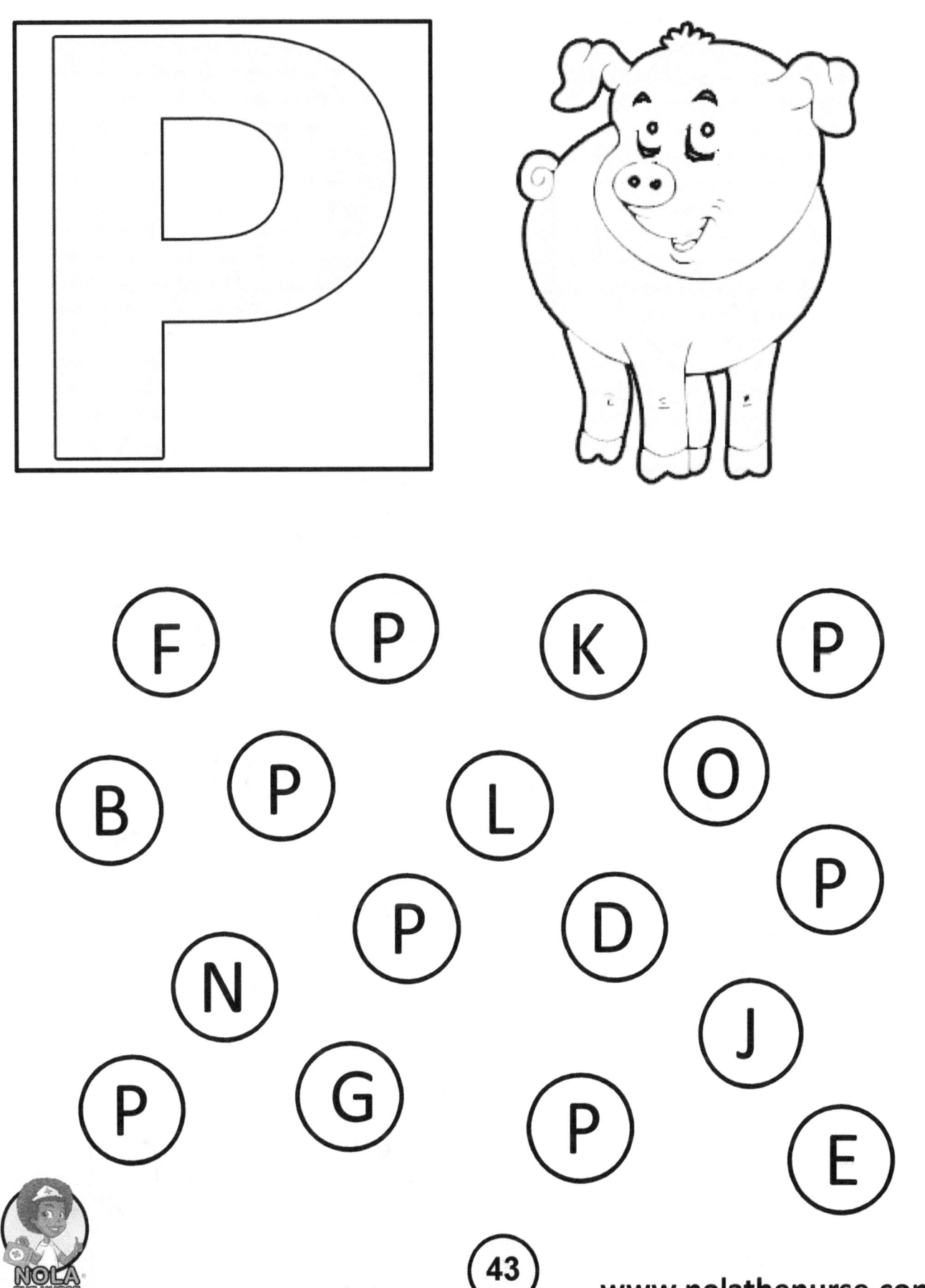

Activity sheet Letter Q.

Activity sheet Letter R.

Activity sheet Letter S.

Activity sheet Letter T.

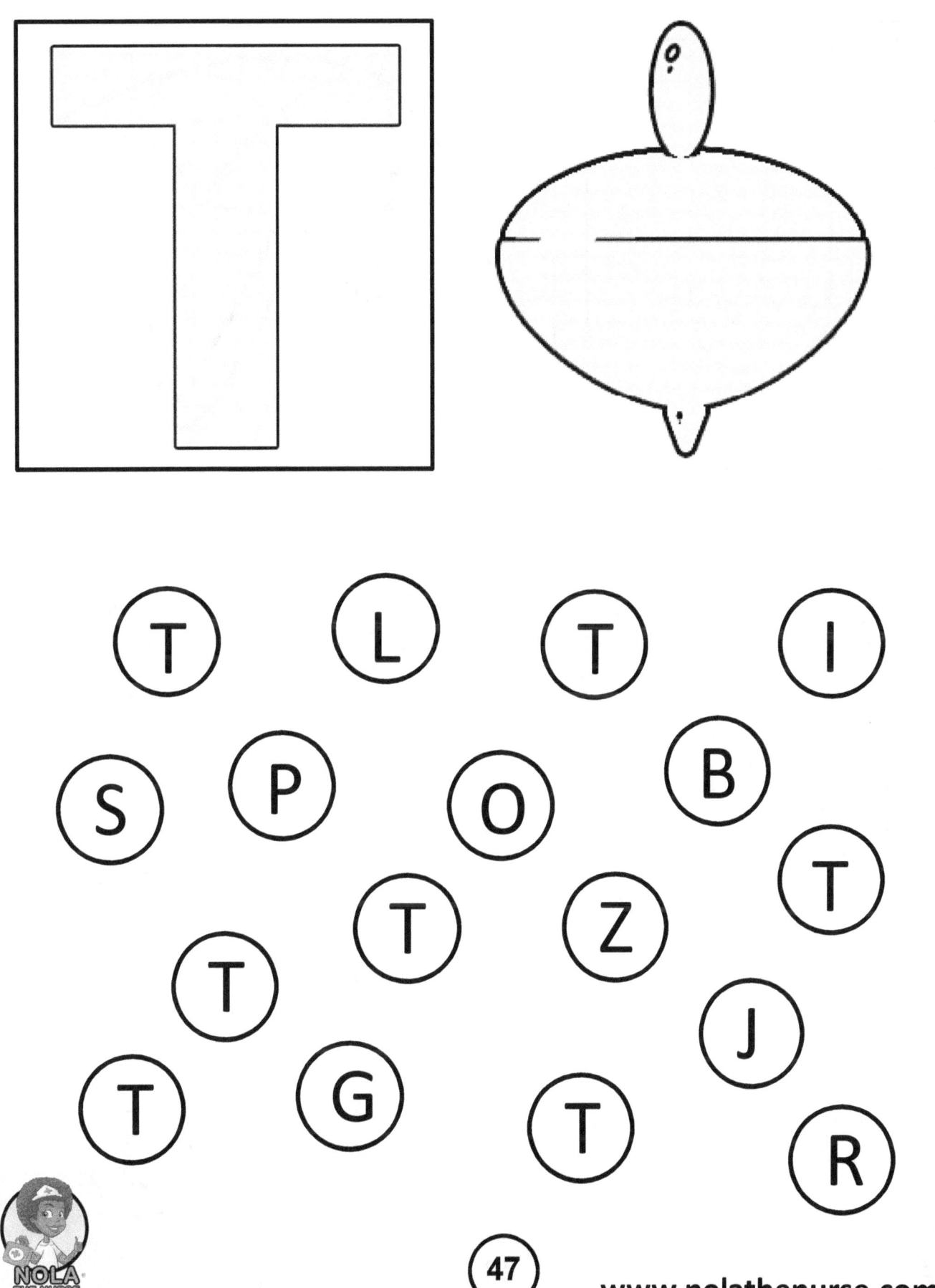

Activity sheet Letter U.

Activity sheet Letter V.

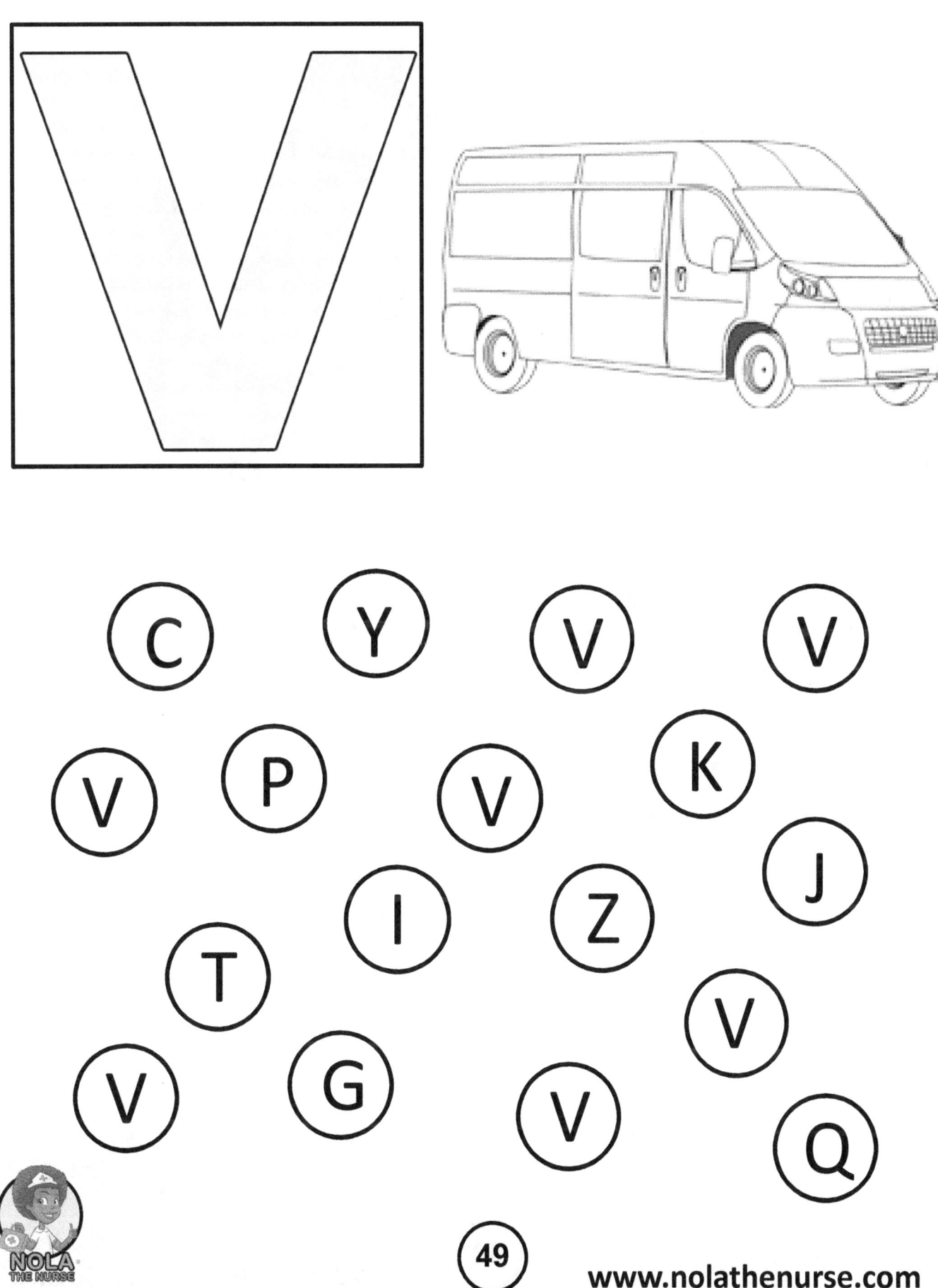

Activity sheet Letter W.

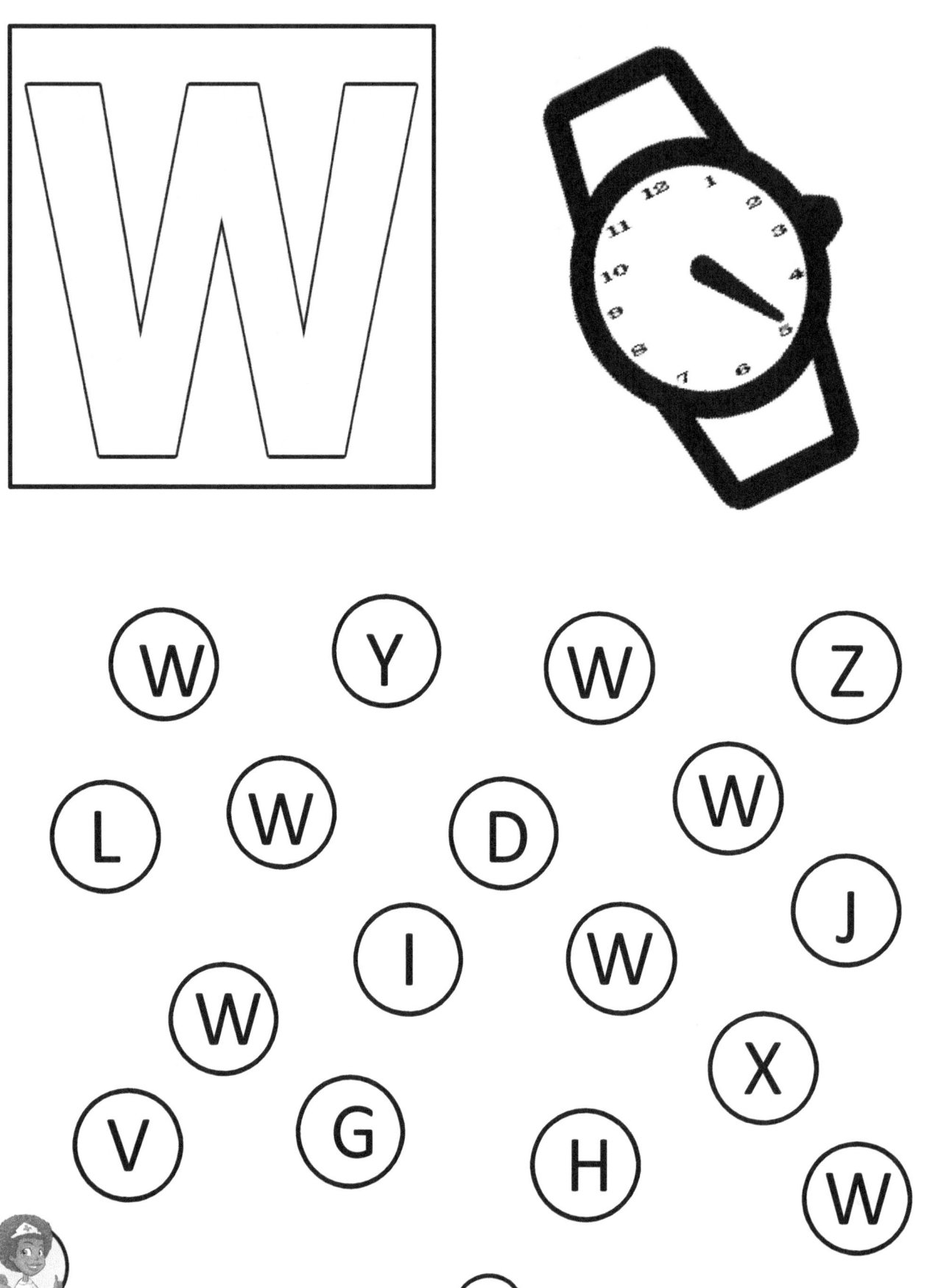

Activity sheet Letter X.

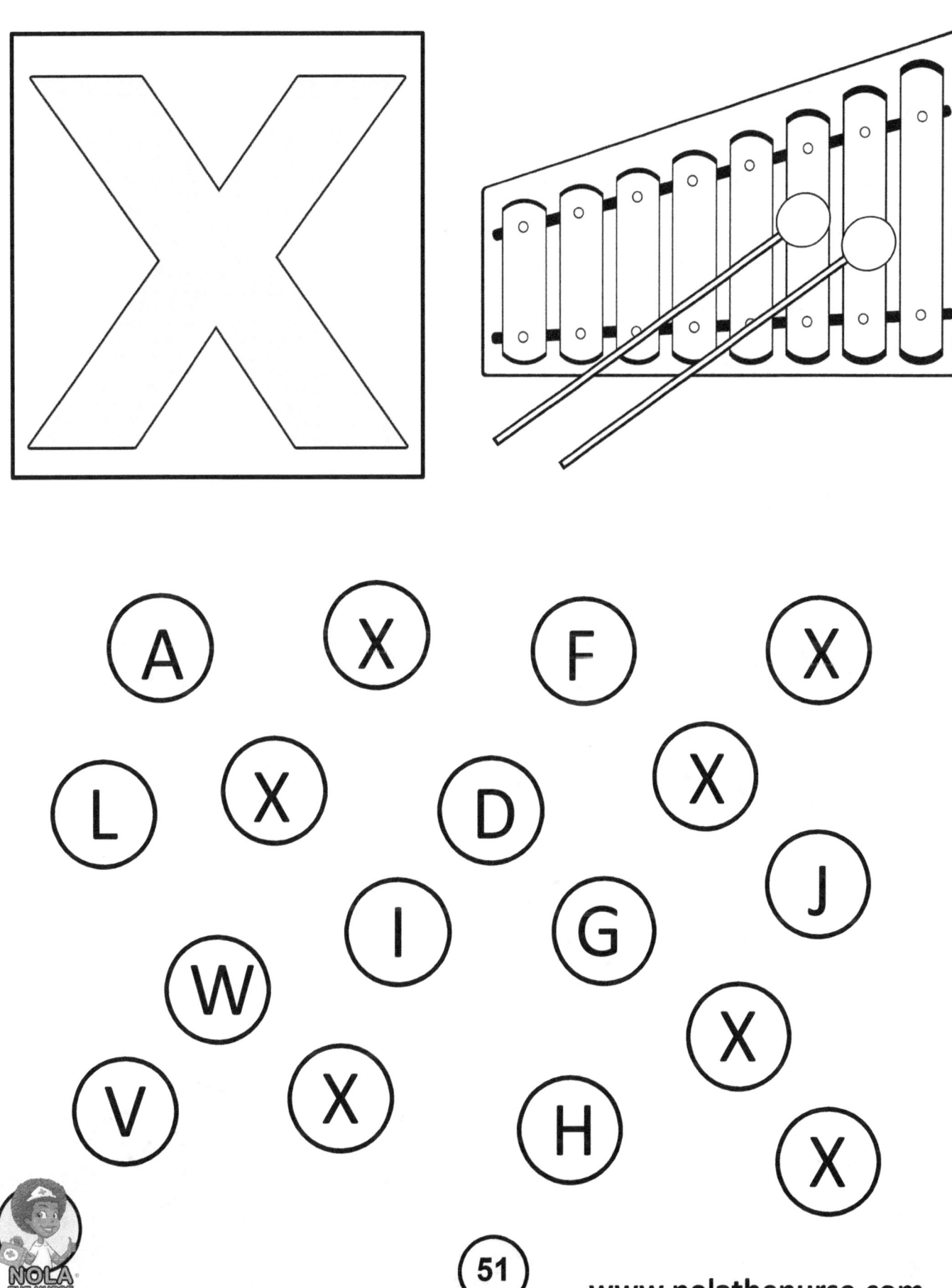

Activity sheet Letter Y.

Activity sheet Letter Z.

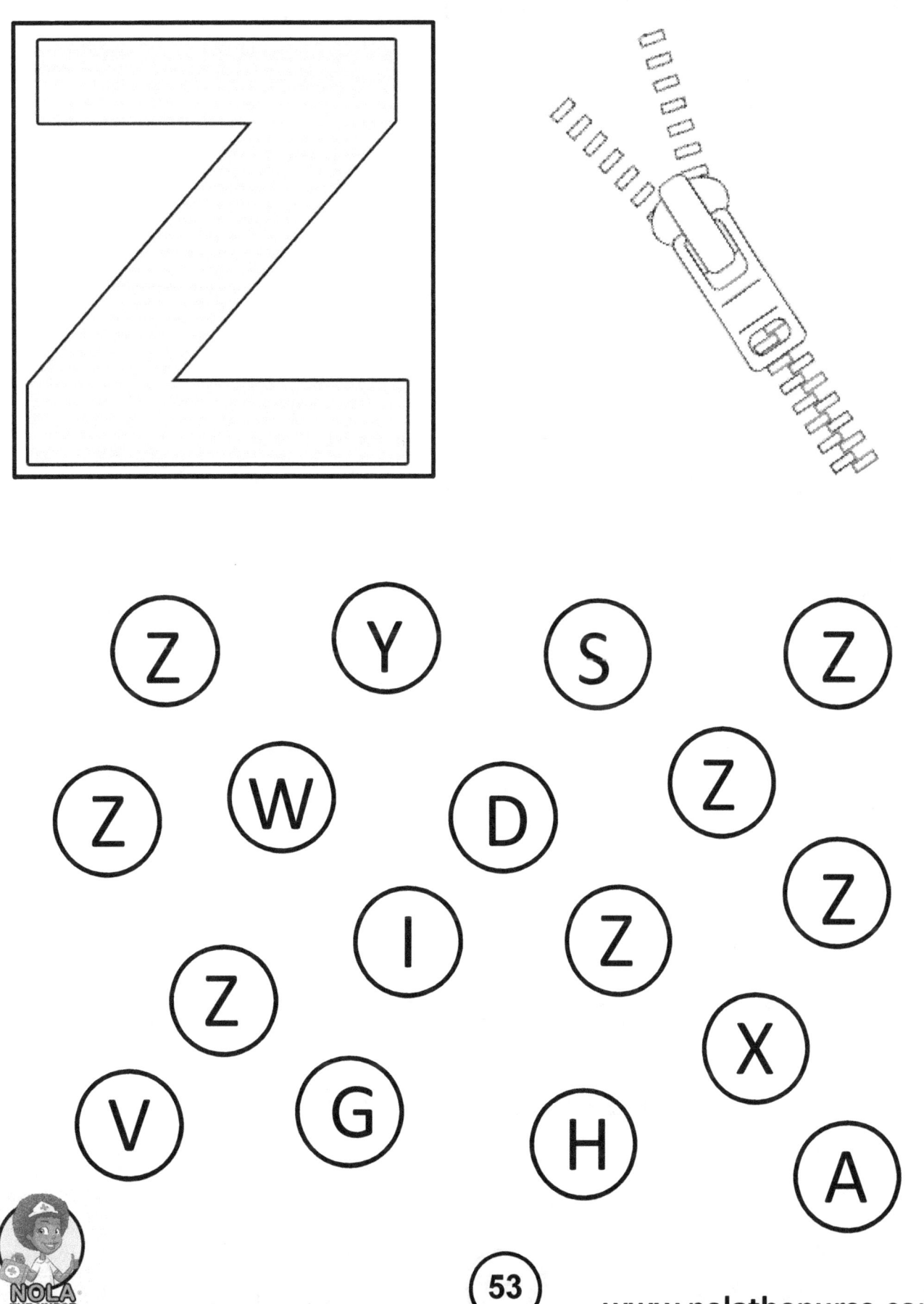

Math Activity Book

Multiple Worksheets for math learners.

Check the largest in each box.

Name : -

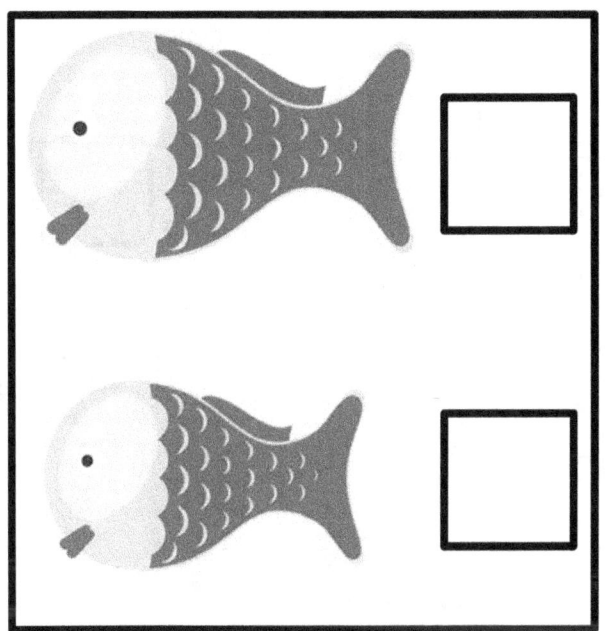
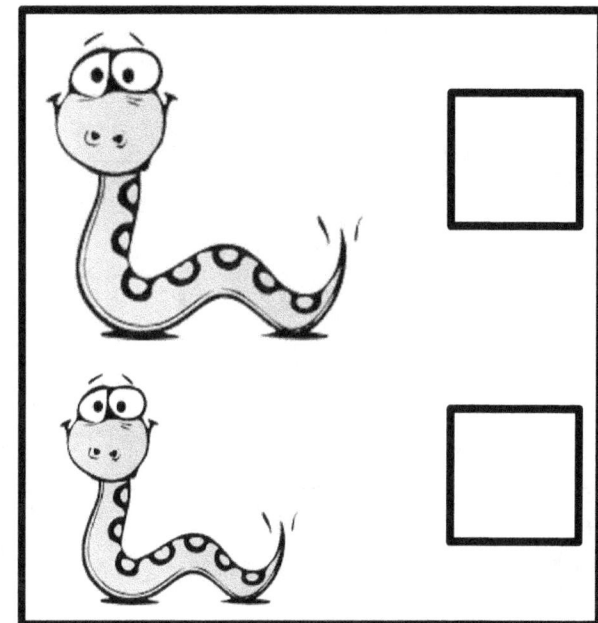

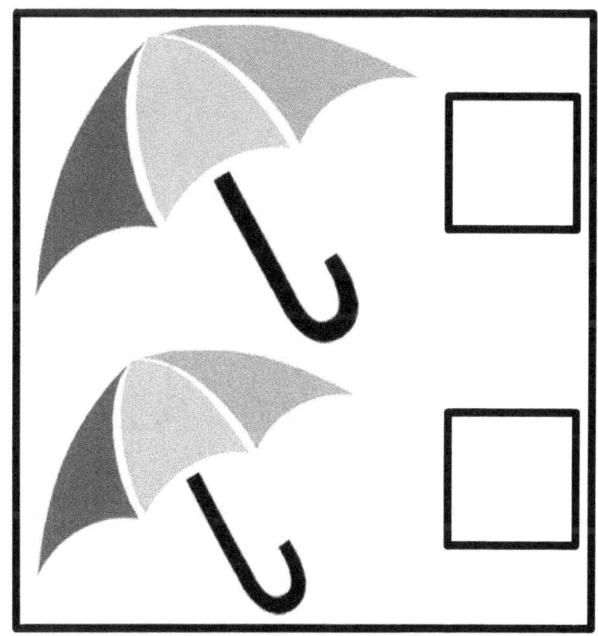

Check the smallest in each box.

Name : -

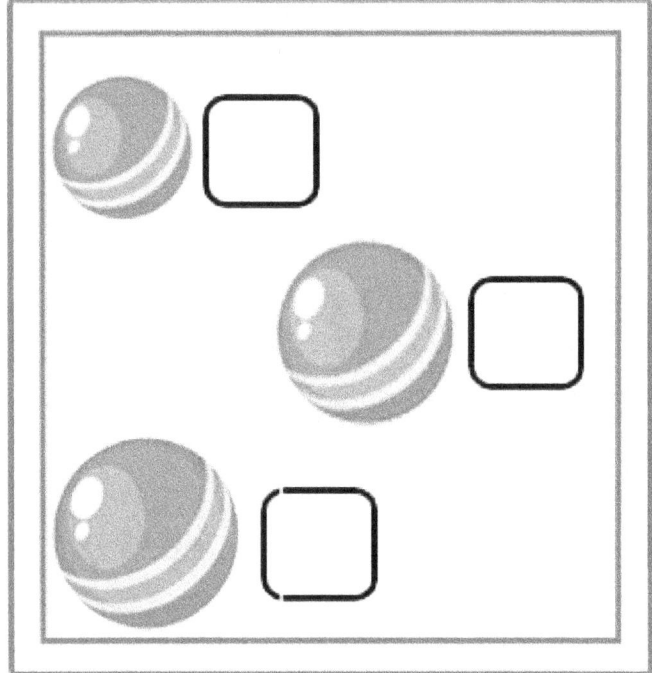
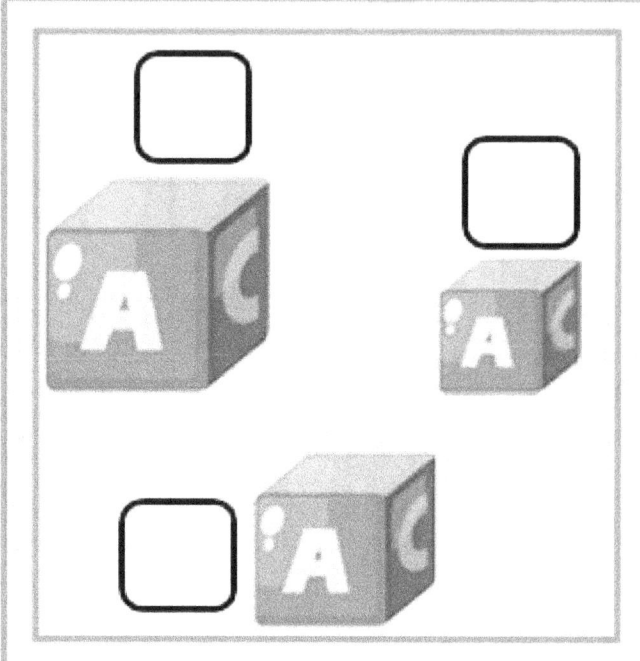
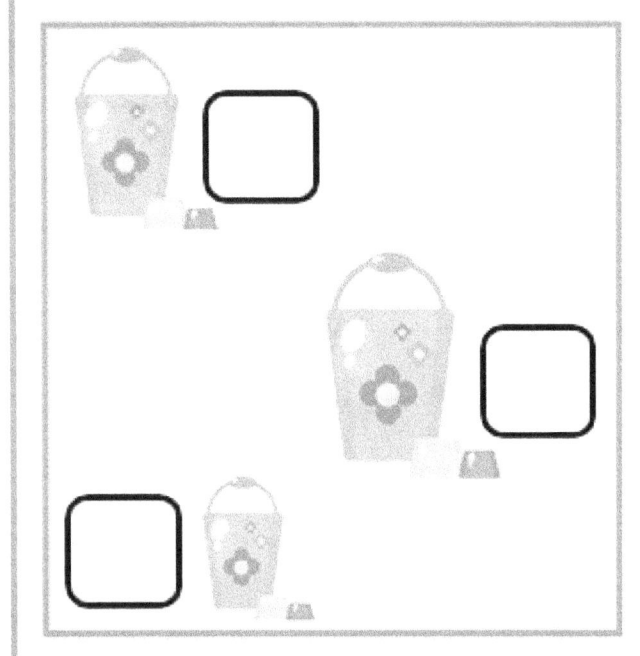
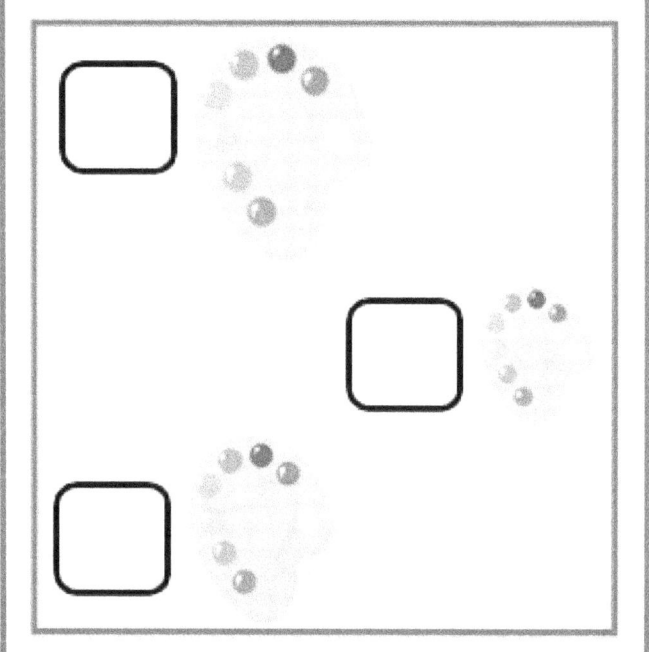

Write Forward Counting.

Name : -

1	2			5
	7		9	
11		13		15
	17		19	
			24	25
26	27			
		33		
36	37		39	
		43		45
46			49	

Write Backward Counting.

Name : -

50	49			46
	44		42	
		38		36
	34		32	
		28		26
25	24			
		18		
15	14		12	
		8		6
5			2	

Cut and Paste

Name : -

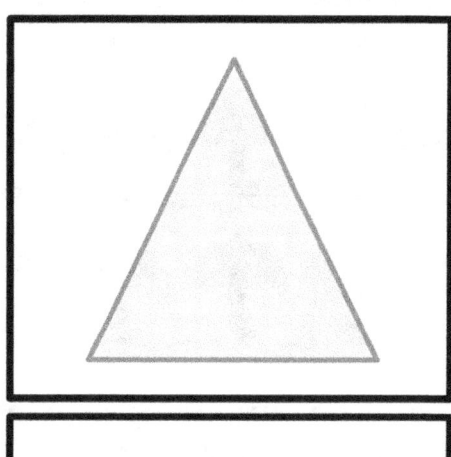

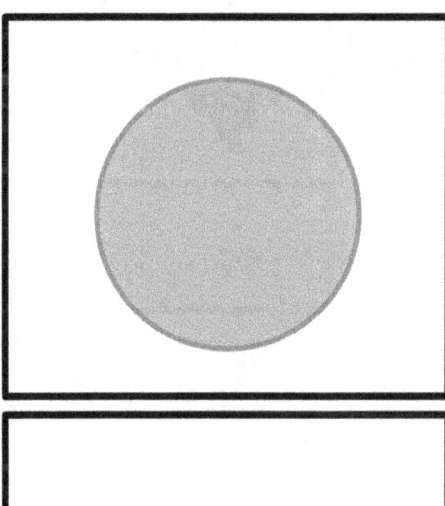

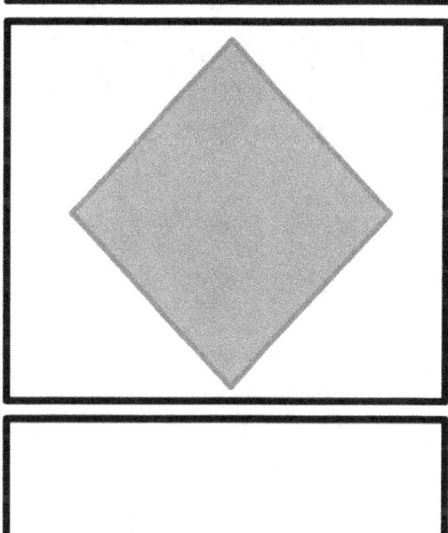

Circle	Triangle
Diamond	Square

www.nolathenurse.com

Count and Write

Name : -

(umbrellas) ☂ × 28 [ ]

(hearts) ♥ × 25 [ ]

(yin-yang) ☯ × 24 [ ]

Write the numbers in order from Least to Greatest.

Name : -

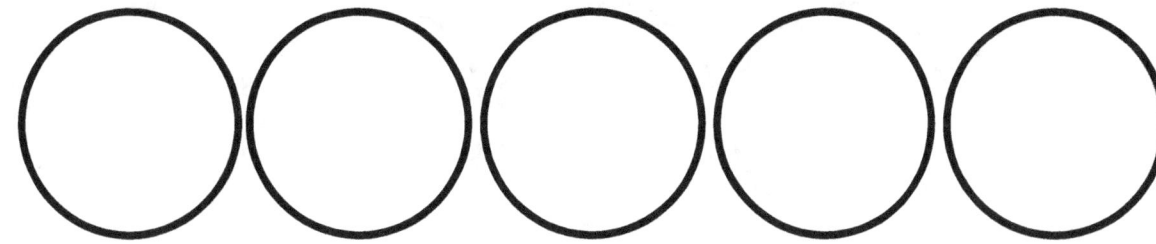

57, 35, 28, 80, 17

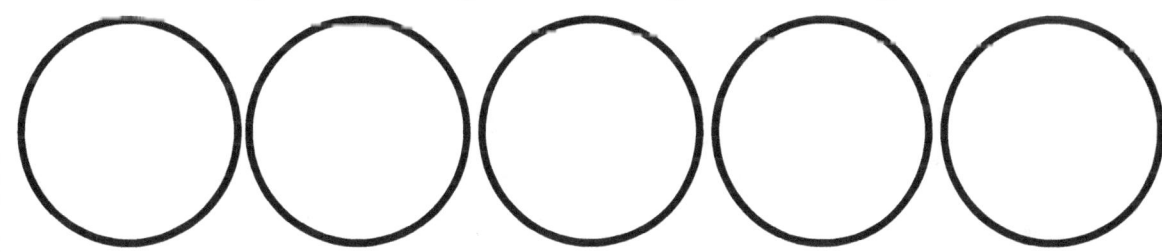

43, 82, 37, 89, 06

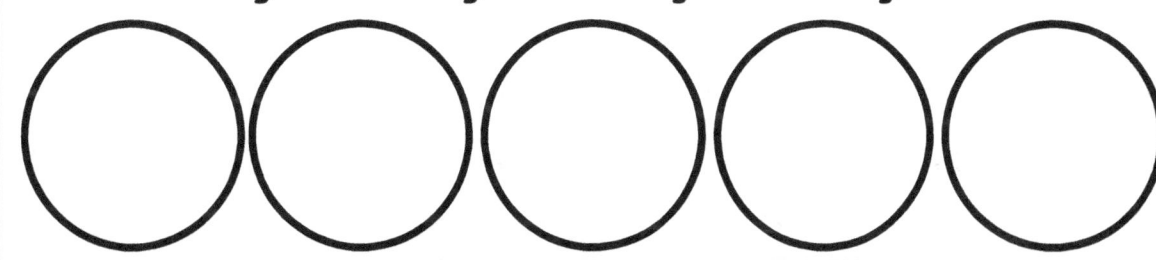

71, 61, 50, 33, 99

Write the numbers in order from Greatest to Least.

Name : -

09, 25, 56, 90, 32

○ ○ ○ ○ ○

54, 69, 12, 88, 47

○ ○ ○ ○ ○

11, 34, 72, 93, 61

○ ○ ○ ○ ○

62

www.nolathenurse.com

Less Than, Equal To, Greater Than <, =, >

Name : - _____

47 ☐ 47	09 ☐ 18
25 ☐ 56	81 ☐ 59
11 ☐ 11	44 ☐ 63
83 ☐ 98	35 ☐ 35
67 ☐ 39	02 ☐ 20

www.nolathenurse.com

Counting By Fives

Name : -

5		15		25
	75		85	
	10	15		
35		45		55
	85		95	

Read the number and draw the circles in ten frames.

Name : -

6 | ● | ● | ● | ● | ● |
  | ● | | | | |

3

8

7

4

Count the objects and color the right number box.

Name : -

Color the Shapes.

Name : -

Color the Rectangle shape.

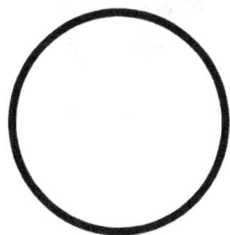  

Color the Circle shape.

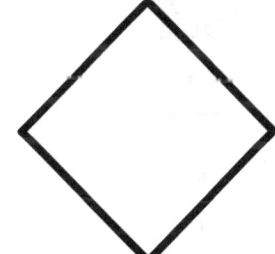 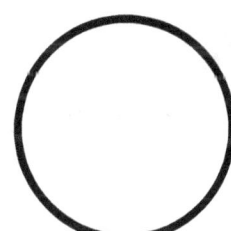 

Color the Hexagon shape.

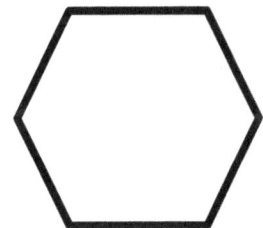  

www.nolathenurse.com

Read the number and draw the missing dots.

Name : - _____

8
2
5

7
4
9

3
6
1

68
www.nolathenurse.com

Draw and Color the Shapes.

Name : -

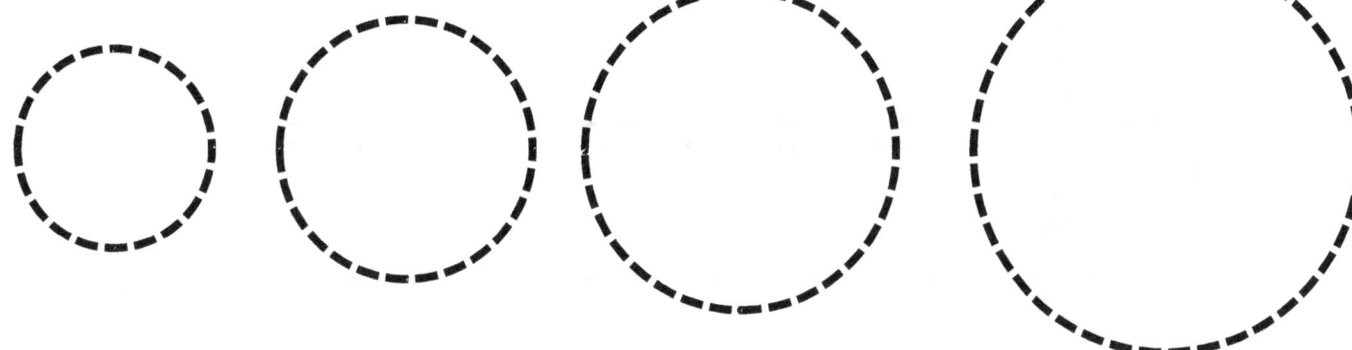

www.nolathenurse.com

Write Number Names

Name : -

1	One
2	
3	
4	
5	
6	
7	
8	
9	
10	

Count the sides of each shape and color the number.

Name : -

| 3 | 4 | 0 | | 1 | 6 | 3 |

| 0 | 7 | 5 | | 4 | 8 | 9 |

| 7 | 8 | 6 | | 5 | 2 | 4 |

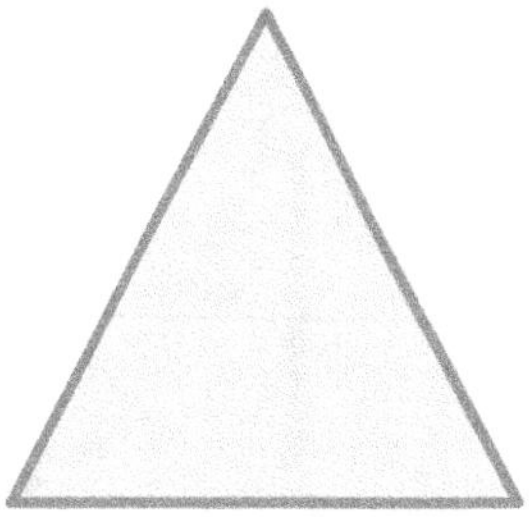

www.nolathenurse.com

What Time Is It ?

Name : -

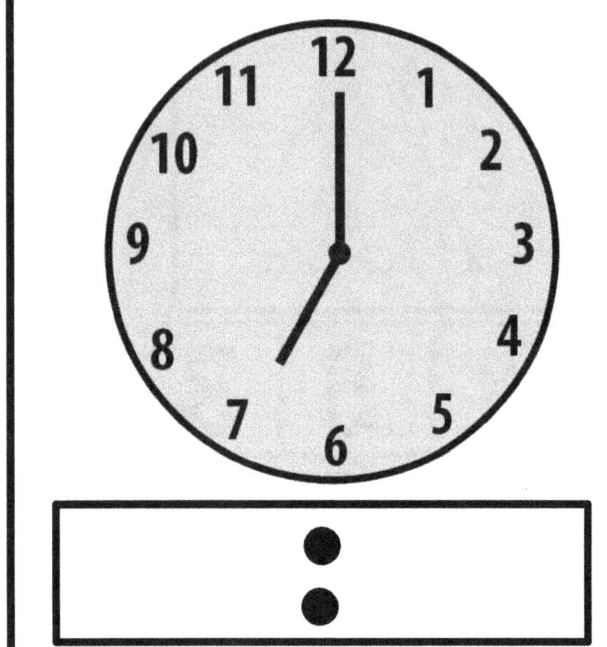
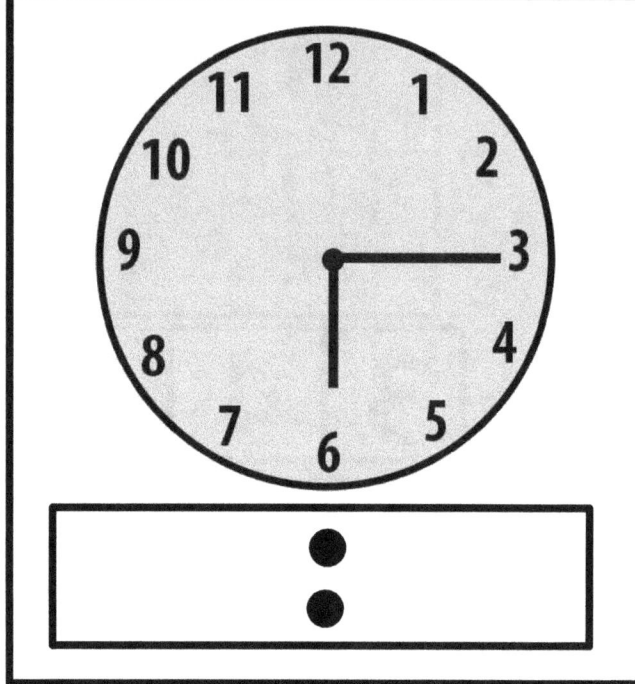
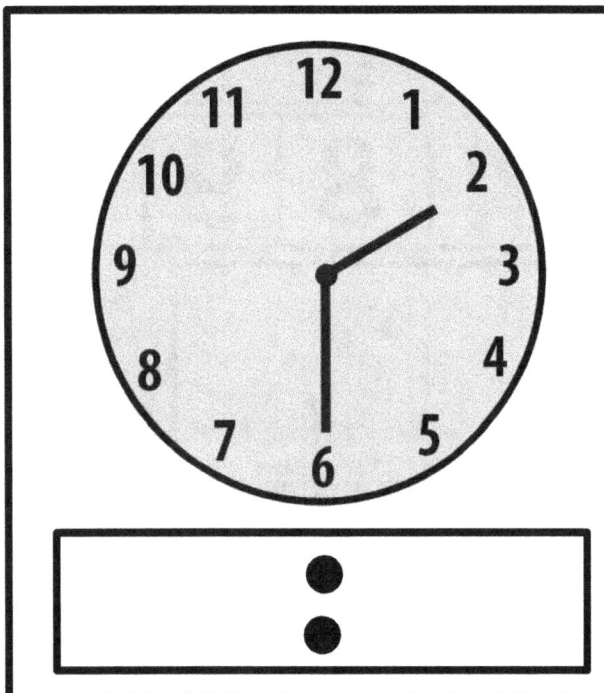
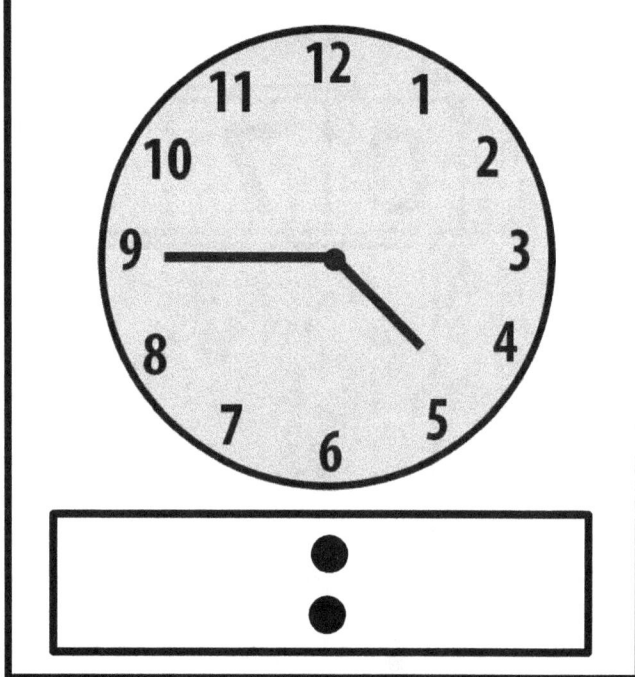

What Comes Before ?

Name : -

	25		56
	68		39
	85		17
	73		92
	44		09

What Comes After?

Name : - _____

15		34	
89		61	
76		55	
43		98	
27		01	

(74)

www.nolathenurse.com

What Comes Before And After ?

Name : -

	25			54	
	08			39	
	13			67	
	86			91	
	72			44	

What Comes Between?

Name : -

14		16	33		35
01		03	59		61
84		86	44		46
29		31	55		57
13		15	94		96

Is It Greater ?

Name : -

Greater than 50	Less than 50

75	39	42	18	06
25	64	87	91	53

www.nolathenurse.com

Is It Lesser ?

Name : -

Less than 50	Greater than 50

39	85	61	27	04
43	62	77	56	18

Cut the half shapes and paste them to make some more shape.

Name : -

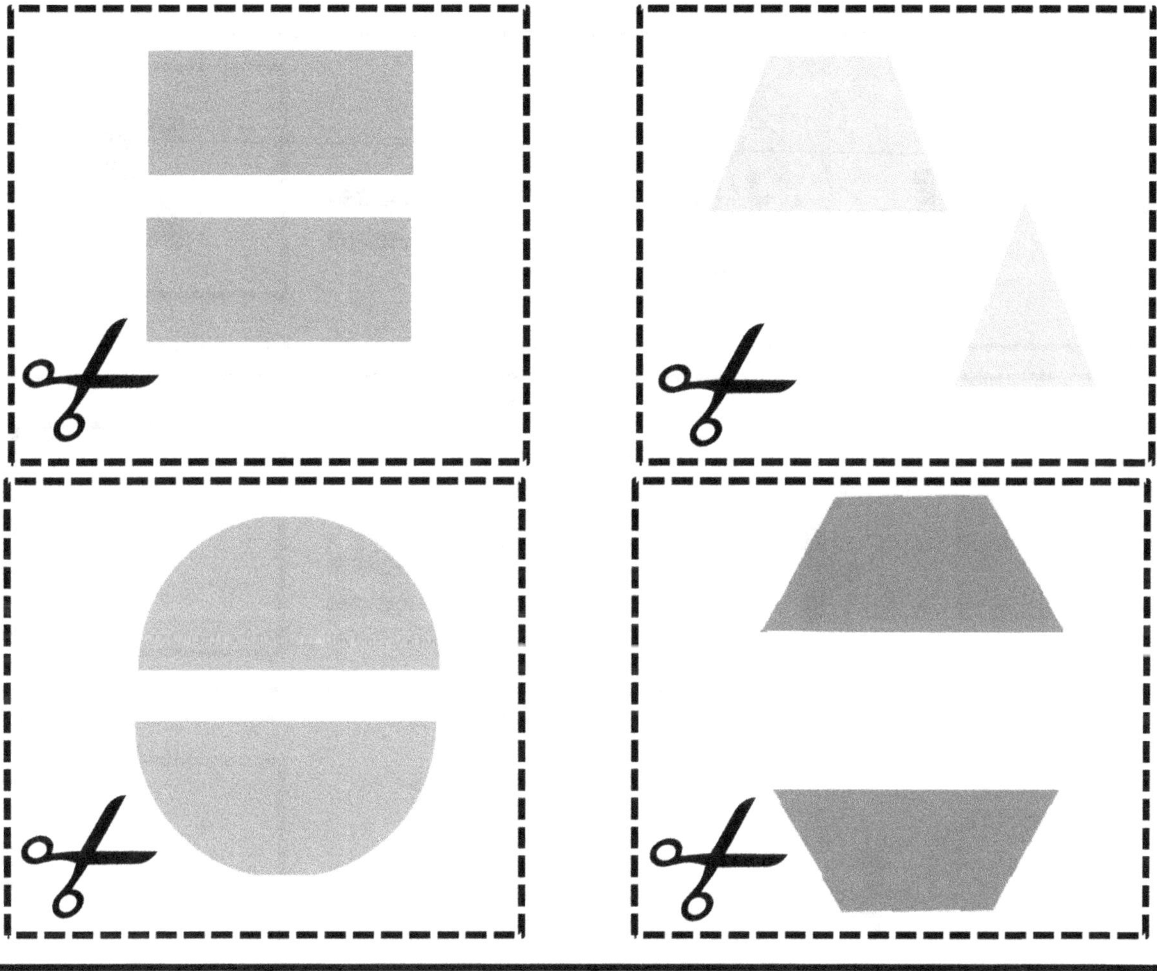

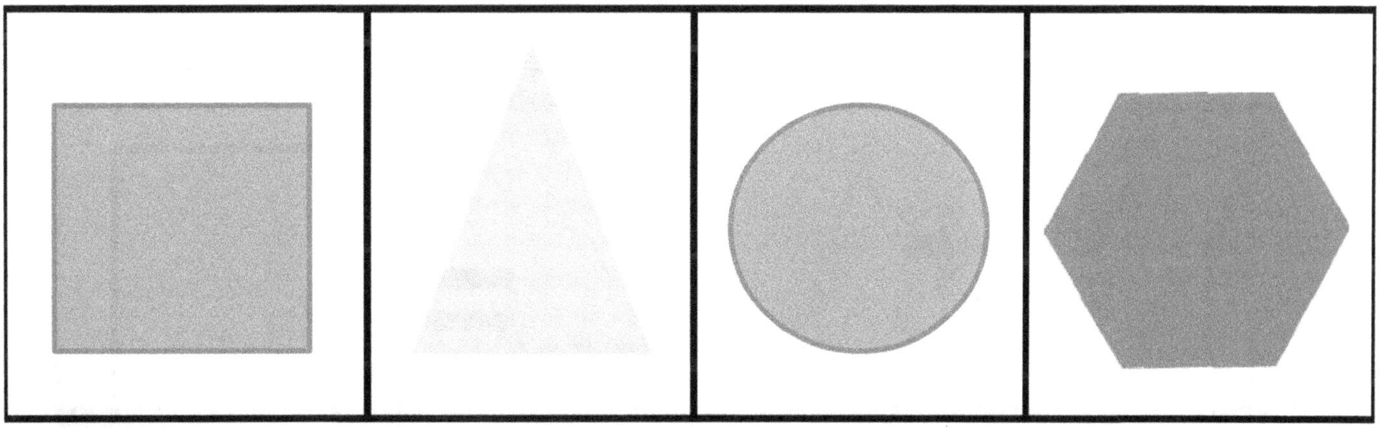

Pictorial Addition

Name : -

🍎 + 🍎 = 2

⭐⭐ + ⭐ = ☐

🧺🧺 + 🧺🧺 = ☐

🎻🎻🎻 + 🎻🎻 = ☐

www.nolathenurse.com

Addition

Name : - _____

4 + 1 _____ _____	6 + 3 _____ _____
3 + 3 _____ _____	5 + 3 _____ _____
8 + 2 _____ _____	1 + 1 _____ _____

(81) www.nolathenurse.com

Addition Bonds

Name : -

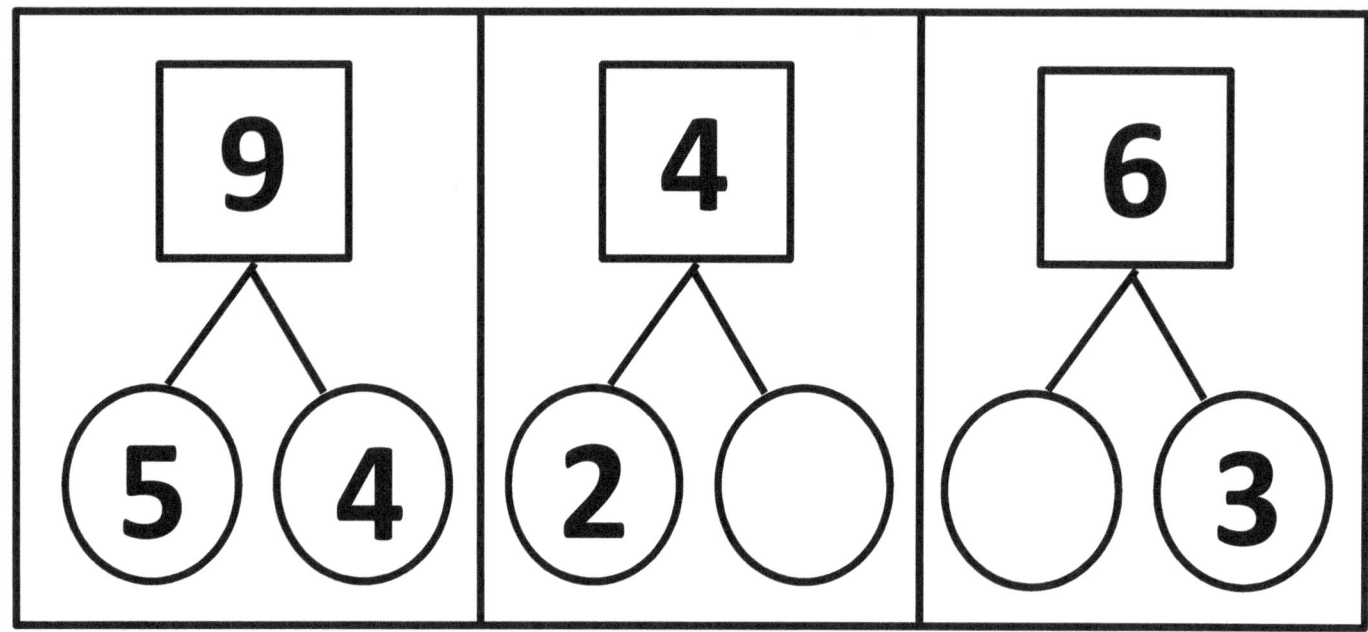

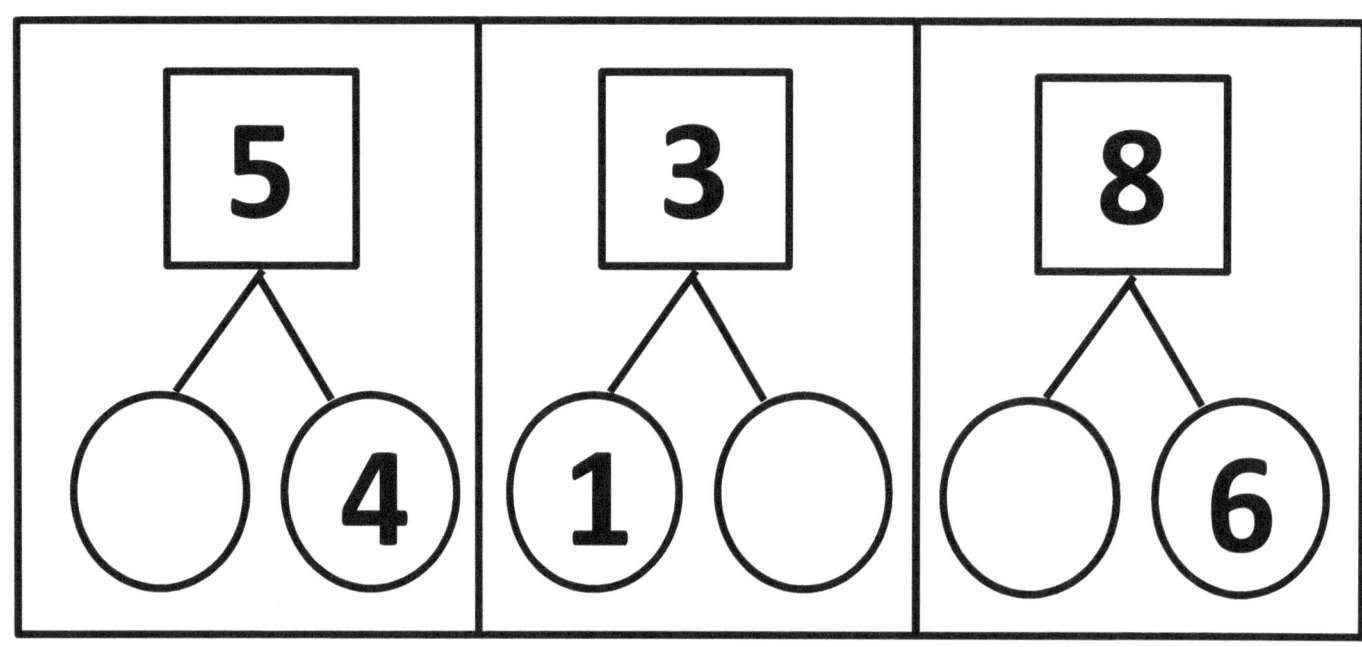

Quick Addition

Name : - _____

5 + 3 = 8	4 + 7 =
7 + 5 =	9 + 6 =
2 + 1 =	5 + 4 =
9 + 6 =	8 + 2 =
3 + 8 =	1 + 9 =
6 + 6 =	5 + 8 =

(83) www.nolathenurse.com

Color the frames to match the number.

Name : -

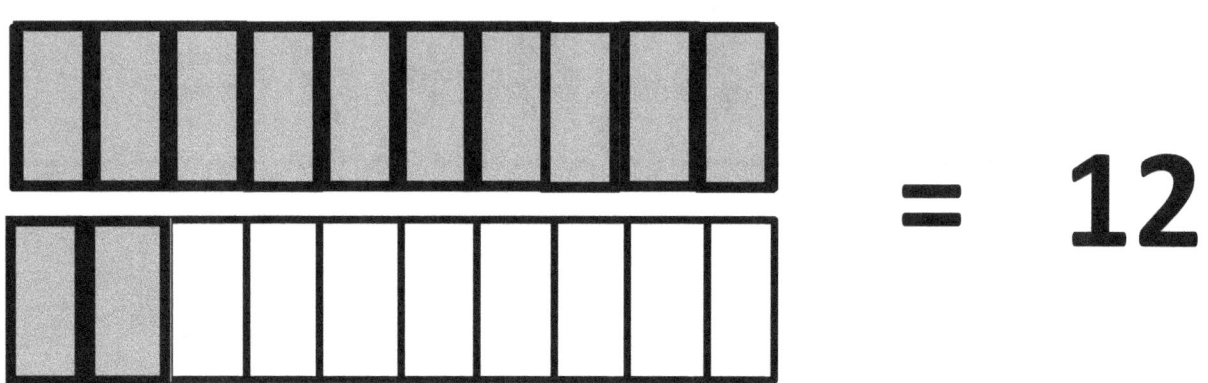

= 12

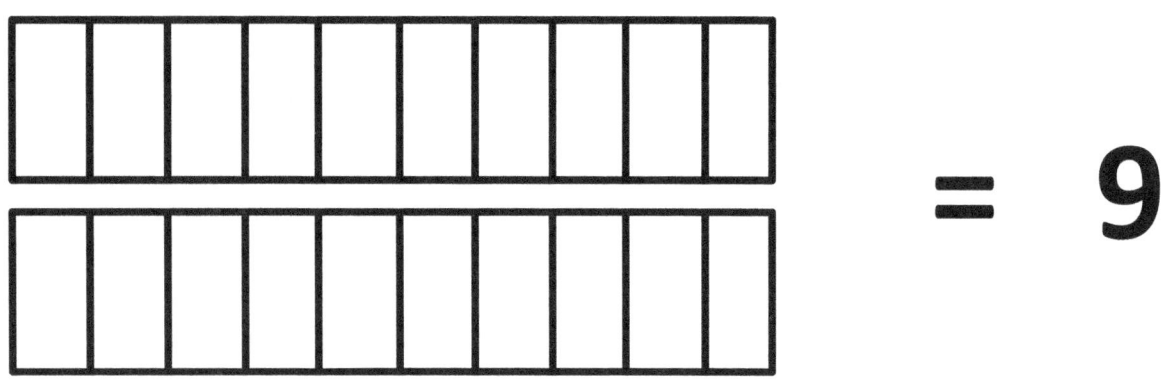

= 9

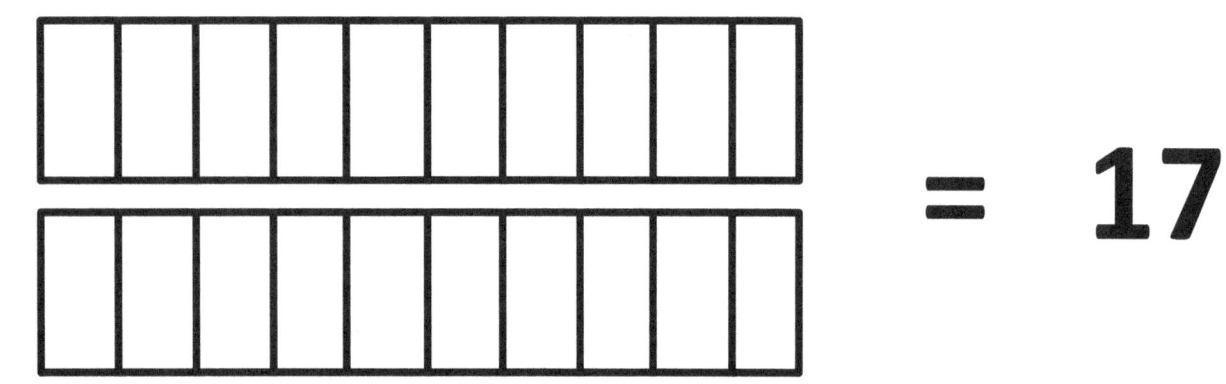

= 17

Write the Missing Number

Name : -

7 + 3 = 10	4 + _ = 20
_ + 5 = 15	_ + 8 = 17
2 + _ = 8	5 + _ = 38
9 + _ = 13	8 + _ = 27
_ + 8 = 18	_ + 9 = 43
6 + _ = 13	_ + 8 = 50

Pictorial Subtraction

Name : -

 = 0

 =

 =

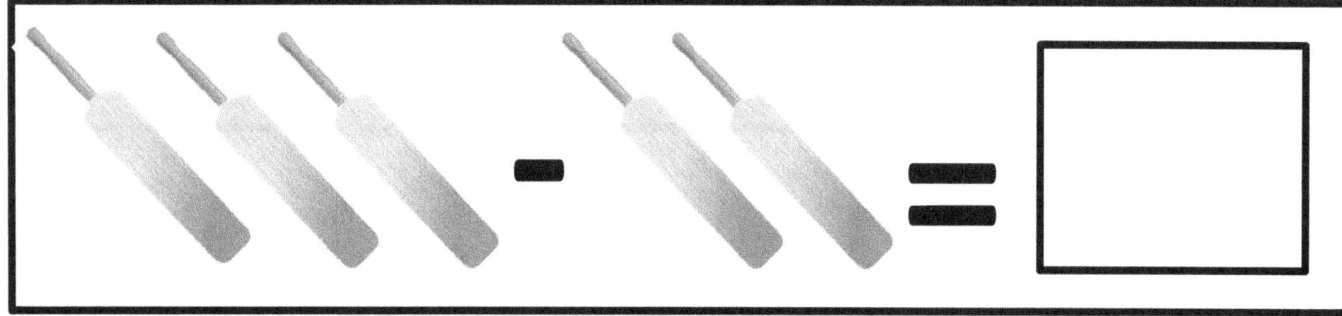 =

Subtraction

Name : - _____

5 - 3 ――― ―――	9 - 5 ――― ―――
4 - 4 ――― ―――	6 - 2 ――― ―――
7 - 1 ――― ―――	8 - 3 ――― ―――

Quick Subtraction

Name : -

5 - 3 = 2	7 - 4 =
7 - 5 =	3 - 1 =
2 - 1 =	5 - 4 =
9 - 6 =	8 - 2 =
8 - 8 =	1 - 1 =
6 - 2 =	4 - 3 =

www.nolathenurse.com

Subtraction Problem

Name : -

3 - 1 = ___

7 - 5 = ___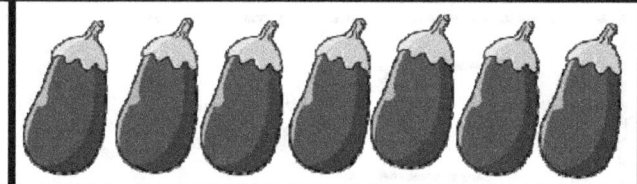

2 - 1 = ___

4 - 3 = ___

6 - 4 = ___

5 - 2 = ___

www.nolathenurse.com

Addition Or Subtraction
Fill in the missing sign [+ , -]

Name : - _____

5 ☐ 2 = 3	3 ☐ 3 = 6
7 ☐ 3 = 10	5 ☐ 4 = 1
6 ☐ 1 = 7	1 ☐ 1 = 2
8 ☐ 5 = 3	2 ☐ 6 = 8
4 ☐ 4 = 0	7 ☐ 4 = 3
9 ☐ 1 = 8	6 ☐ 2 = 4

Find and Color the same Apple

Name : - ☐

More Or Less

Name : -

Color the Dragon with more nails.

Color the Butterfly with less spots.

www.nolathenurse.com

Lets play a Game

Name : - _____

10 **HOME**	Go back to 7	**9**	**8**
Fishing Time Miss a turn	**6**	**7**	**Minus** (-) Go back to 4
5	**Add** (+) Move up to 7	**4**	**3**
0 → START	**1**	**2**	Wear a cap! Miss a turn

(93)   www.nolathenurse.com

These following free color sheets are placed here to help you get to know the characters from the Nola The Nurse® children's book series. Enjoy and pick up a copy of the hottest selling children's book in America that was recently featured on The Harry Show!

Dr. Eden Nurse Practitioner

Nola The Nurse®

Anita

Dr. Baker Nurse Practitioner

Adar

Maddi the Midwife

More books by Dr. Baker

Nola The Nurse® She's On The Go Series Vol 1
Nola The Nurse® & Friends Explore The Holi Fest She's On The Go Series Vol 2
Nola The Nurse® & Friends Explore The Holi Fest She's On The Go Series Vol 2 Coloring Book
Nola The Nurse® Remembers Hurricane Katrina Special Edition
Nola The Nurse® Remembers Hurricane Katrina Special Edition Coloring Book
Black Dot
Nola The Nurse® English/Sight Worksheets for Kindergarten Vol 4
Nola The Nurse® Math Worksheets for Kindergarten Vol 3
Nola The Nurse® Activity Book for Kindergarten Vol 2
Nola The Nurse® Preschool Activity Book Vol 1
Nola The Nurse® Math Worksheets for First Graders Vol 6

Upcoming Titles:
Nola The Nurse® STEM Activity Book for 5-8 year olds Vol 7

www.NolaTheNurse.com
DrBaker@NolaTheNurse.com

About the Author

Dr. Scharmaine L. Baker, NP is a nationally recognized and award-winning nurse practitioner in New Orleans, Louisiana. She has received numerous honors and awards for her contributions to healthcare in New Orleans since she became a family nurse practitioner in 2000, including the 2013 Healthcare Hero award (New Orleans City Business magazine) and 2008 Entrepreneur of the Year award (ADVANCE for Nurse Practitioner magazine).

Dr. Baker has a doctor of nursing practice (DNP) degree from Chatham University in Pittsburgh, PA, and she is a fellow of the American Association of Nurse Practitioners (AANP). She was inspired to make house calls while caring for her grandmother, who was ill and needed an in-home doctor.

After Hurricane Katrina, Dr. Baker was instrumental in caring for the sick and disabled in New Orleans, where hospitals had closed and doctors had evacuated but never returned. Her patient load went from 100 to 500 in only three months. Thanks to her passion and unwavering dedication to caring for homebound patients in her home town, Dr. Baker's story was featured on the CBS Evening News with Katie Couric.

Today, Dr. Baker maintains a busy private practice in New Orleans by making house calls to the elderly and disabled who would otherwise not receive healthcare.

When this award-winning and nationally known nurse practitioner is not on the road delivering keynote speeches and attending various other media events, she loves reading to her children, Skylar Rose and Wyatt Shane.

www.DrBakerNP.com
www.NolaTheNurse.com
https://shop.nolathenurse.com

www.ingramcontent.com/pod-product-compliance
Lightning Source LLC
Chambersburg PA
CBHW081353080526
44588CB00016B/2476